"This series is a tremendous resource for t
understanding of how the gospel is wov(
pastors and scholars doing gospel busines
logical feast preparing God's people to apply the entire Bible to all of life,
wholly committed to Christ's priorities."

    BRYAN CHAPELL, President Emeritus, Covenant Theological Seminary; Senior Pastor,
    Grace Presbyterian Church, Peoria, Illinois

"Mark Twain may have smiled when he wrote to a friend, 'I didn't have time to write you a
short letter, so I wrote you a long letter.' But the truth of Twain's remark remains serious and
universal, because well-reasoned, compact writing requires extra time and extra hard work.
And this is what we have in the Crossway Bible study series *Knowing the Bible*. The skilled
authors and notable editors provide the contours of each book of the Bible as well as the
grand theological themes that bind them together as one Book. Here, in a 12-week format,
are carefully wrought studies that will ignite the mind and the heart."

    R. KENT HUGHES, Visiting Professor of Practical Theology, Westminster Theological
    Seminary

"*Knowing the Bible* brings together a gifted team of Bible teachers to produce a high-quality
series of study guides. The coordinated focus of these materials is unique: biblical content,
provocative questions, systematic theology, practical application, and the gospel story of
God's grace presented all the way through Scripture."

    PHILIP G. RYKEN, President, Wheaton College

"These *Knowing the Bible* volumes provide a significant and very welcome variation on the
general run of inductive Bible studies. This series provides substantial instruction, as well as
teaching through the very questions that are asked. *Knowing the Bible* then goes even further
by showing how any given text links with the gospel, the whole Bible, and the formation of
theology. I heartily endorse this orientation of individual books to the whole Bible and the
gospel, and I applaud the demonstration that sound theology was not something invented
later by Christians, but is right there in the pages of Scripture."

    GRAEME L. GOLDSWORTHY, former lecturer, Moore Theological College; author,
    According to Plan, Gospel and Kingdom, The Gospel in Revelation, and *Gospel and Wisdom*

"What a gift to earnest, Bible-loving, Bible-searching believers! The organization and
structure of the Bible study format presented through the *Knowing the Bible* series is so well
conceived. Students of the Word are led to understand the content of passages through per-
ceptive, guided questions, and they are given rich insights and application all along the way
in the brief but illuminating sections that conclude each study. What potential growth in
depth and breadth of understanding these studies offer! One can only pray that vast numbers
of believers will discover more of God and the beauty of his Word through these rich studies."

    BRUCE A. WARE, Professor of Christian Theology, The Southern Baptist Theological
    Seminary

KNOWING THE BIBLE

J. I. Packer, Theological Editor
Dane C. Ortlund, Series Editor
Lane T. Dennis, Executive Editor

•   •   •   •   •   •

Genesis	Psalms	Jonah, Micah, and Nahum	Ephesians
Exodus	Proverbs		Philippians
Leviticus	Ecclesiastes	Haggai, Zechariah, and Malachi	Colossians and Philemon
Numbers	Song of Solomon		1–2 Thessalonians
Deuteronomy	Isaiah	Matthew	1–2 Timothy and Titus
Joshua	Jeremiah	Mark	
Judges	Lamentations, Habakkuk, and Zephaniah	Luke	Hebrews
Ruth and Esther		John	James
1–2 Samuel		Acts	1–2 Peter and Jude
1–2 Kings	Ezekiel	Romans	1–3 John
1–2 Chronicles	Daniel	1 Corinthians	Revelation
Ezra and Nehemiah	Hosea	2 Corinthians	
Job	Joel, Amos, and Obadiah	Galatians	

•   •   •   •   •   •

J. I. PACKER is Board of Governors' Professor of Theology at Regent College (Vancouver, BC). Dr. Packer earned his DPhil at the University of Oxford. He is known and loved worldwide as the author of the best-selling book *Knowing God*, as well as many other titles on theology and the Christian life. He serves as the General Editor of the ESV Bible and as the Theological Editor for the *ESV Study Bible*.

LANE T. DENNIS is President of Crossway, a not-for-profit publishing ministry. Dr. Dennis earned his PhD from Northwestern University. He is Chair of the ESV Bible Translation Oversight Committee and Executive Editor of the *ESV Study Bible*.

DANE C. ORTLUND is Executive Vice President of Bible Publishing and Bible Publisher at Crossway. He is a graduate of Covenant Theological Seminary (MDiv, ThM) and Wheaton College (BA, PhD). Dr. Ortlund has authored several books and scholarly articles in the areas of Bible, theology, and Christian living.

EPHESIANS

A 12-WEEK STUDY

Eric C. Redmond

WHEATON, ILLINOIS

Knowing the Bible: Ephesians, A 12-Week Study

Copyright © 2016 by Crossway

Published by Crossway
        1300 Crescent Street
        Wheaton, Illinois 60187

Some content used in this study guide has been adapted from the *ESV Study Bible*, copyright © 2008 by Crossway, pages 2257–2274. Used by permission. All rights reserved.

Cover design: Simplicated Studio

First printing 2016

Printed in the United States of America

Trade paperback ISBN: 978-1-4335-4845-1
EPub ISBN: 978-1-4335-4848-2
PDF ISBN: 978-1-4335-4846-8
Mobipocket ISBN: 978-1-4335-4847-5

Crossway is a publishing ministry of Good News Publishers.

VP		29	28	27	26	25	24	23	22	21	20	19
16	15	14	13	12	11	10	9	8	7	6	5	4

TABLE OF CONTENTS

SERIES PREFACE

KNOWING THE BIBLE, as the series title indicates, was created to help readers know and understand the meaning, the message, and the God of the Bible. Each volume in the series consists of 12 units that progressively take the reader through a clear, concise study of that book of the Bible. In this way, any given volume can fruitfully be used in a 12-week format either in group study, such as in a church-based context, or in individual study. Of course, these 12 studies could be completed in fewer or more than 12 weeks, as convenient, depending on the context in which they are used.

Each study unit gives an overview of the text at hand before digging into it with a series of questions for reflection or discussion. The unit then concludes by highlighting the gospel of grace in each passage ("Gospel Glimpses"), identifying whole-Bible themes that occur in the passage ("Whole-Bible Connections"), and pinpointing Christian doctrines that are affirmed in the passage ("Theological Soundings").

The final component to each unit is a section for reflecting on personal and practical implications from the passage at hand. The layout provides space for recording responses to the questions proposed, and we think readers need to do this to get the full benefit of the exercise. The series also includes definitions of key words. These definitions are indicated by a note number in the text and are found at the end of each chapter.

Lastly, to help understand the Bible in this deeper way, we urge readers to use the ESV Bible and the *ESV Study Bible*, which are available in various print and digital formats, including online editions at esv.org. The Knowing the Bible series is also available online.

May the Lord greatly bless your study as you seek to know him through knowing his Word.

J. I. Packer
Lane T. Dennis

WEEK 1: OVERVIEW:
THE CHURCH IN
GOD'S PLAN

The audience of Ephesians was well-known to the apostle Paul (Acts 19). For two years the disciples in Ephesus observed Paul daily reasoning about the kingdom of God and teaching the Scriptures (Acts 19:8–10). This ministry resulted in a gospel witness spreading throughout the Roman province of Asia. The message of Christ reached those practicing dark arts and worshiping Artemis in this great ancient city, where demonic[1] influence was strong.

Paul explains these believers' formation into a church as the work of Christ alone. The decree of God always included the formation of the beautiful bride of Christ—the body of Christ, of which Christ is the head.

Ephesians concerns the mystery of the church in the plan of God. The letter calls believers to walk in love, holiness, and wisdom within their local church congregation and in the world. Paul reveals that this mystery concerns earthly, present matters, as well as matters in the invisible realm, both in the present world and in the world to come. (For further background, see the ESV *Study Bible*, pages 2257–2261; available online at esv.org.)

Placing It in the Larger Story

The Lord revealed the inclusion of Gentiles in his plan of salvation when he called Abram and made promises to bless all nations through him (Gen. 12:1–3). From the beginnings of the Lord's dealings with Israel, Gentiles came to the God of Israel—as when Rahab and Ruth left their gods to follow him.

Even though Israel as a whole rejected their Messiah,[2] Jesus told his initial Jewish followers that he would build the church and that they would have a significant role in its growth (Matt. 16:18). In doing so, he indicated that something new had dawned in the messianic age—an assembly, "my church," distinguished from greater Israel. The book of Acts shows that soon after the church's formation, Gentiles joined the assembly without converting to Judaism or following the Mosaic law. The inclusion of the Gentiles into the largely Jewish church raised strong feelings among both believing and unbelieving Jews (Acts 11:1–3; 21:20–25).

Ephesians explains the theology of the inclusion of those formerly outside the covenant with Israel. Believing Jews and Gentiles in Ephesus are part of a larger design. The church will transform the marriages, work, parenting, and morality of her members. She will become the true temple of God.

Key Verse

"We are his workmanship, created in Christ Jesus for good works, which God prepared beforehand, that we should walk in them" (Eph. 2:10).

Date and Historical Background

Paul wrote Ephesians during his first imprisonment (3:1; 4:1; 6:20). He is therefore writing in AD 62, about five years after his final meeting with the elders of this assembly (Acts 20:17–35). Christianity is still in its infancy, being only a thirty-year-old movement. Unlike other New Testament letters, one does not discern any error, conflict, or misunderstanding that prompts the writing of this letter. Paul writes simply to advance Christian insight and maturity.

Outline

I. Believers' Spiritual Blessings in Christ in God's Plan (1:1–14)

II. Prayer for Revelation about the Blessings in Christ the Head (1:15–23)

III. Mercy Making the Dead Alive by Grace (2:1–10)

As You Get Started

Read the book of Ephesians as if it were a letter from the apostle Paul written to your own church. What stands out as unique or significant as you read? Write down your initial thoughts.

vv 19-22
A call for unity as one church. Paul gives specifics on how to achieve this and why it is necessary

Two prayers and one request for prayer in Ephesians each revolves around revelation and mystery (1:15–22; 3:14–21; 6:18–20). What might this tell you about Paul's hope for believers who read Ephesians?

That they would have an inward heart revelation through the Spirit of the Magnitude of God's love thru Christ.
eart — eyes of your heart (1:18)
oul — inner being (3:16)
ind — able to comprehend (3:14) to know (3:19)

9

In reading Ephesians, what words and ideas are repeated? How might you group some of these words and ideas together under larger headings that point to Paul's main idea in Ephesians?

GRACE
MYSTERY
SPIRIT
IN CHRIST
LOVE

> ## As You Finish This Unit . . .

Using the prayer of Ephesians 1:17–23, take a few minutes to ask the Lord to reveal to you and your church more and more of his will for his glory as you begin this study of Ephesians.

Definitions

[1] **Demon** – An evil spirit that can inhabit a human being and influence him or her to carry out its will. Demons are fallen angels, created by God and always limited by him. Jesus and his followers cast out many demons, demonstrating Jesus' superiority over them. All demons will one day be destroyed along with Satan (Matt. 25:41; Rev. 20:10).

[2] **Messiah** – Transliteration of a Hebrew word meaning "anointed one," the equivalent of the Greek word *Christ*. Originally applied to a person specially designated for a particular serving role, such as king or priest. Jesus himself affirmed that he was the Messiah sent from God (Matt. 16:16–17).

WEEK 2: BELIEVERS' SPIRITUAL BLESSINGS

Ephesians 1:1–14

▲

The Place of the Passage

Paul begins Ephesians by revealing that the church is a spiritual entity initiated and formed by Christ, leading to a social identity of earthly relationships. The blessings of the church's heavenly identity become the basis for the new kind of conduct Paul exhorts the church to practice.

The Big Picture

Ephesians 1:1–14 shows that the church is part of the plan of God from all eternity. God forms the church in Christ to bring himself glory. This is a demonstration of God's grace[1] based on the work of Christ and intended to accomplish God's will both here on earth and in heaven.

Reflection and Discussion

Read through Ephesians 1:1–14 and make note of significant words and concepts. Then review the questions below concerning this introductory section to Ephesians' discussion of the church and write your notes on them. (For further background, see the *ESV Study Bible*, pages 2262–2263; available online at esv.org.)

1. Apostolic Greeting and Initiation of Themes (1:1–2)

Paul writes to this church as an "apostle[2] of Christ Jesus by the will of God." What authority does his designation as "apostle" give to this writing? What might the phrases "of Christ Jesus" and "by the will of God" say about the motive of the writing? Why will the combination of this motive and authority be important to the remainder of this letter?

The believers who comprise this church are identified as "saints" who reside "in Ephesus." How does the first term influence the second? How should a local congregation view itself in light of what "saints" means in relationship to both the Lord and fellow believers?

Paul calls this church "faithful in Christ Jesus" and communicates grace and peace to them from God. What sort of relationship with God is indicated by a judgment of their faithfulness? Why might such a congregation need grace and peace from the Father and Jesus Christ?

----

2. Revelation of Spiritual Blessings in Christ from the Father (1:3–10)

"Blessed be" denotes that Paul is offering praise to God for the spiritual blessings listed in the verses to follow. The blessings are anchored "in Christ"—in his person and work in salvation—and "in the heavenly places." List the spiritual blessings "in" and "through" Christ mentioned in 1:4–6. What defining boundaries do "in Christ" and "in the heavenly places" place on "chosen in him," "predestined,"[3] and "adopted"?

Paul includes "redemption"[4] and "forgiveness of our trespasses" among the blessings lavished upon believers by grace. What does this working of grace indicate about the Ephesians' previous and current condition?

Several terms indicate the Lord's intentions for spiritual blessings: "that we should be," "in love" (1:4), "to the praise of his glorious grace" (1:6), and "to unite all things in him" (1:10). These intentions align with God's eternal will (or "purpose" or "plan"; 1:1, 5, 9, 10). How would you summarize the earthly and eternal goals of the work of Christ in the church and for every believer?

3. Revelation of Spiritual Blessings in Christ through the Spirit (1:11–14)

In 1:11, "in him," "predestined," "purpose," and "will" carry over previously mentioned truths related to the believers' spiritual blessings. According to these truths, how do believers gain an inheritance in Christ? What is the goal of this inheritance, and why might it carry special significance for those "who were the first to hope in Christ"?

The work of Christ in redemption, which began in eternity past, includes the sealing of the Holy Spirit. Hearing the truth of the gospel actualizes this sealing (1:13). What role, then, does belief play in the entire tapestry of salvation discussed in 1:3–14? What assurance of salvation does the working of the Spirit provide?

Read through the following three sections on *Gospel Glimpses, Whole-Bible Connections*, and *Theological Soundings*. Then take time to consider the *Personal Implications* these sections may have for you.

Gospel Glimpses

FORGIVENESS. As sinners we have offended God, broken his laws, disobeyed his commands, and rebelled against his will. This puts enmity between our Maker and us. If this breach is not repaired, the sinner remains in jeopardy of punishment from God. However, in the death and resurrection of Christ, the Lord himself has provided for our forgiveness. (Matt. 27:28). It is an act of his grace toward us (Eph. 1:7–8).

ATONEMENT. Although mentioned directly only once in 1:3–14, the death of Christ is the centerpiece of spiritual blessing. As the Levitical code states, "It is the blood that makes atonement by the life" (Lev. 17:11; see Heb. 9:22). Christ's life-giving act provided the blood sacrifice that atones for the sins of believers. The cross of Christ is central to all the spiritual blessings we read about in Ephesians.

Whole-Bible Connections

GOD'S DECREE. Terms in Ephesians 1:1–14 such as "will," "purpose," "plan," and "counsel" reveal that God has a decree from eternity that cannot be altered or thwarted (Prov. 21:30). As ruler of the universe and eternity, he controls the outcomes of all things, bringing them to their completion. That doesn't mean our own choices don't matter; we still must exercise our will and believe in him (Eph. 1:13). Yet God's decree establishes the entire plan of salvation for the church. The decree guarantees that God will obtain glory for the full working of salvation (1:6,

12, 14), which will include the final sanctification of believers (1:4, 14). This is the fulfillment of the plan that God announced in the garden of Eden (Gen. 3:15). The disobedience of Israel and the church, whatever form it may take, will not at any stage truncate the plan of salvation, because God's decree remains in force (Rom. 8:28; 11:29). This planned togetherness of Jews and Gentiles in the church was not clearly revealed prior to Paul and his fellow apostles (Eph. 3:4–10); hence God calls it a "mystery," meaning a secret previously hidden but now revealed (1:9–10).

INHERITANCE. God's promise to Israel was that they would be his "treasured possession among all peoples" (Ex. 19:5; Deut. 7:6; 26:18; Mal. 3:17) and he would give them a land (Gen. 15:18–21; Ex. 3:8; Deut. 26:1–3). Peter reveals that all believers in Christ share this same promise of being the inheritance of God (1 Pet. 2:5–9). Through the work of Christ, believers receive the inheritance of Christ himself and the riches of eternity (Eph. 1:11, 14, 18; Heb. 9:15; 1 Pet. 1:4).

Theological Soundings

ELECTION. Just as the Lord lovingly chose Israel from among the nations as his own people (Deut. 7:7–8; 10:15; Hos. 11:1; Mal. 1:2), so in mercy the Lord lovingly has chosen those he will save from all the people of the earth (Rom. 9:11–13; Eph. 1:4–5). This choice is part of his eternal decree, occurring before the creation of the world or any of its inhabitants (Eph. 1:5; 2:10). The choice is *in Christ*, not man; therefore, it does not rest on any foreseen decision of any human person (2:9). Gloriously, in his act of election, God chooses to save people who deserve his greatest wrath and who would otherwise never choose to come to him. Election is the only way anyone receives salvation in Christ. Those who are chosen will experience God's eternal mercy (Rom. 8:29–30).

GUARANTOR. When the Lord wished to assure Abraham that he would receive the promised inheritance, the Lord himself sealed the covenant, making the promises depend on his character alone (Gen. 15:7–21). Similarly, in order to guarantee the work of salvation from beginning to end, the Lord gives the Spirit of God as the guarantor (or down payment) of our inheritance. The presence of the indwelling Spirit in believers secures salvation for the elect forever. It guarantees that those predestined to be holy and blameless will not lose the gift of Christ but will acquire its full possession.

Personal Implications

Take time to reflect on the implications of Ephesians 1:1–14 for your own life today. Ponder what the Lord is doing in you to bring glory to himself. Make notes below on the personal implications for your walk with the Lord of the (1) *Gospel Glimpses*, (2) *Whole-Bible Connections*, (3) *Theological Soundings*, and (4) this passage as a whole.

15

1. Gospel Glimpses

_____

_____

_____

_____

_____

2. Whole-Bible Connections

_____

_____

_____

_____

_____

3. Theological Soundings

_____

_____

_____

_____

_____

4. Ephesians 1:1–14

_____

_____

_____

_____

_____

▶ As You Finish This Unit . . .

Take a moment now to ask for the Lord's blessing and help as you continue in this study of Ephesians. And take a moment also to look back through this unit of study, to reflect on some key things that the Lord may be teaching you—and perhaps to highlight and underline these things to review again in the future.

Definitions

[1] **Grace** – Unmerited favor, especially the free gift of salvation that God gives to believers through faith in Jesus Christ.

[2] **Apostle** – Means "one who is sent" and refers to one who is an official representative of another. In the NT, refers specifically to those whom Jesus chose to represent him.

[3] **Predestination** – God's sovereign choice of people for redemption and eternal life. Also referred to as "election."

[4] **Redemption** – In the context of the Bible, the act of buying back someone who had become enslaved or something that had been lost to someone else. Through his death and resurrection, Jesus purchased redemption for all believers (Col. 1:13–14).

WEEK 3: PRAYER FOR REVELATION

Ephesians 1:15–23

The Place of the Passage

Paul states that all that the Lord has done for the church in Christ is a mystery now being revealed (Eph. 1:9). However, without the working of the Lord to reveal his will, much of the significance of these spiritual blessings will remain hidden and ineffective in the life of a local assembly. Paul therefore prays for illumination.

The Big Picture

In Ephesians 1:15–23, Paul's prayer moves from the mode and objects of prayer to a request for revelation. The prayer has as its focus the fullness of Christ in the church.

> ### Reflection and Discussion

Read through the entire text for this study, Ephesians 1:15–23. Then interact with the following questions and record your notes on them concerning this section of Ephesians. (For further background, see the *ESV Study Bible*, pages 2263–2264; available online at esv.org.)

1. Reason, Manner, and Object of Paul's Prayer for Revelation (1:15–17)

The spiritual blessings granted in Christ and the report of the believers' faith in Christ and love for all believers give Paul reason to pray. If the Lord has provided every spiritual blessing in Christ in the heavenly places, and many in Ephesus have believed on Christ, why does knowledge of these two truths move Paul to pray?

b/c he is thankful and prays a trinitarian protection over their pursuits. w/ spirit led wisdom.

If the Ephesians already show love like Christ, what does Paul's ongoing prayer for them tell us about demonstrating Christ's love?

we demonstrate Christ's love only through the spirit who guides us in wisdom and keeps us close to the knowledge of Christ.

The believers at Ephesus were included in Paul's prayers for more than 10 years (from AD[1] 55 until his death in about 68). What does this say about Paul's priorities for the church and for his own life? <u>What does this necessity of continual prayer for revelation indicate about the spiritual blessings in the lives of believers?</u>

That they & he would stay anchored in the knowledge of Christ and atuned to the spirit.

One finds the phrase "God of our Lord Jesus Christ" elsewhere in Paul's writings (Rom. 15:6; 2 Cor. 11:31; Col. 1:3). "Father of glory" harkens back to the glory of God in Ephesians 1:6, 12, and 14. What part does each member of the Trinity[2] play in Paul's request for the Ephesians? How do these parts relate to their roles in salvation seen in 1:1–14?

God the Father gives spirit which reminds of the knowledge of Christ. God gives the son, son bring salvation, spirit is given as promise of fulfilling plan.

2. The Focus on Power in Paul's Prayer for Revelation (1:18–20)

Paul asks God to reveal more of himself in wisdom—to give knowledge that will change believers through the power of what the Trinity has done for us in Christ. What is the significance of the figure of speech used in asking for "eyes of the heart" to be "enlightened"?

The prayer itself seeks three outcomes. What are the three formerly mysterious things Paul is asking the Trinity to illuminate for the people in Ephesus? What does a prayer for enlightenment indicate about the knowledge of the will of God in members of this congregation?

Hope of his calling, wealth of his glorious inheritance, & the immeasurable greatness of his power toward us who believe, all according to his strength. He makes known what he wants about himself for his glory.

Much of the remainder of the prayer asks for enlightenment with respect to greatness and strength, the "immeasurable greatness of his power." What type of strength is Paul praying that the church will grasp with the eyes of the heart?

God's power as displayed through Christs death, ressurection, and authority enthroned alongside God.

19

In 1:20 Paul makes reference to Christ's ascension,[3] including Christ's position at the "right hand" of God, a symbol of sovereign rule (Ps. 110:1; Acts 2:33; 1 Pet. 3:22). What, then, is Paul expecting the Spirit to reveal about the power available to believers?

He is athourity above ALL and has conquered sin, satan & death.

3. Praying to See the Headship of Christ (1:21–23)

Christ's exaltation establishes his rule "far above" all governing powers. How should the Ephesians' position in Christ color our thoughts on the church's relationship to earthly ruling powers?

Two additional aspects of Christ's rule relate to names and eras (v. 21). What names of authority on earth might Paul be referencing? What does the scope of "this age" and the "one to come" indicate about the authority of Christ in the history of the church's dealings on earth? What is the future of earthly and spiritual powers?

The placing of "all things" under the feet of Christ makes his power exclusive, as do "all rule," "every name," "this age [and] . . . the age to come," and "all things to the church" (1:22). Yet one does not now see the full expression of this

20

rule. What does the believers' identity as "his body" indicate about how Christ intends to express his headship on earth?

Gospel Glimpses

HOPE. Prior to our salvation, we were doomed to perish. Many attempt to cover such hopelessness with temporal joys and achievements that seek to avoid the inevitability of their own demise. The gospel brings hope—assurance of resurrection and inheritance. Because Christ canceled sin and defeated death, those in him have the certain hope of eternity. Peter describes our hope in Christ as a "living" hope (1 Pet. 1:3).

RESURRECTION. Related to the concept of hope is the resurrection of Christ. Without the resurrection, believers have no more hope than anyone else (1 Cor. 15:14, 17–18). John indicates that the "second death" has no power over those who believe in Christ (John 11:25–26; Rev. 2:11; 20:6, 14; 21:8). Life after death, including a bodily resurrection, is promised to all believers.

Whole-Bible Connections

SANCTIFIED BY PRAYER. In the story of redemption, one sees many of God's leaders praying for his people. Some of these prayers were simple intercessions (Exodus 32). Other prayers displayed a particularly sanctifying tone (1 Kings 8; Daniel 9). The Lord Jesus prayed for the church to be sanctified (John 17). Paul's prayer here in Ephesians 1:15–23 seeks the maturity of the church, as Christians increase in their understanding of their Lord. Prayer is essential to accomplishing the will of God.

GOD AS VICTOR. Christ's exaltation to the right hand of God places him above earthly and cosmic powers in the age that has dawned and in the age to come. As prophesied in the Old Testament, every knee will bow in submission to

Read through the following three sections on *Gospel Glimpses, Whole-Bible Connections*, and *Theological Soundings*. Then take time to consider the *Personal Implications* these sections may have for you.

Christ (Isa. 45:23), he will be the victorious King of glory in battle (Ps. 24:7–10), and he will crush the rebellious nations (Ps. 2:9). These victories will bring an end to the ongoing conflict between the Enemy and the people of God (Gen. 3:15; Ps. 110:1). Christ's rule as head provides for the present and final victory of believers in all conflicts (Rom. 8:37–39).

Theological Soundings

HEADSHIP. Christ's head-body relationship to the church reflects the relationship the Lord had with Israel. The head is the authority, determining the direction and actions of the body. The body willingly submits itself to the head rather than working autonomously or rebelliously. The differing roles are not competitive, nor do they represent advantage or inequality. All spiritual blessings of believers are preplanned works of grace. Paul's return to the metaphor in Ephesians 4:15 and 5:23 suggests that the head-body relationship is implicit throughout the letter.

AUTHORITY OF THE CHURCH. Throughout the history of Christianity, church and earthly authorities have existed largely in conflict with one another. This is true whether we speak of governing authorities that separate church and state jurisdictions or general secular authorities that promote worldviews rejecting the message and morality the church proclaims. Nevertheless, Scripture demonstrates that Christ calls the church to be an expression of his rule in the present world. Yet this means of expression combines moral courage with humble citizenship, unity with love, and holiness with wisdom, so that transformed lives give evidence of the power of the gospel.

Personal Implications

Take time to reflect on the implications of Ephesians 1:15–23 for your own life today. Consider what you have learned that might lead you to praise God, repent of sin, and trust in his gracious promises. Make notes below on the personal implications for your walk with the Lord of the (1) *Gospel Glimpses*, (2) *Whole-Bible Connections*, (3) *Theological Soundings*, and (4) this passage as a whole.

1. Gospel Glimpses

2. Whole-Bible Connections

3. Theological Soundings

4. Ephesians 1:15–23

As You Finish This Unit . . .

Take a moment now to ask for the Lord's blessing and help as you continue in this study of Ephesians. And take a moment also to look back through this unit of study, to reflect on key things that the Lord may be teaching you—and perhaps to highlight and underline these things to review again in the future.

Definitions

[1] **AD** – Abbreviation for *Anno Domini* ("in the year of our Lord"). Refers to the era of history following the birth of Jesus Christ, which immediately follows the era designated BC ("before Christ").

[2] **The Trinity** – The Godhead as it exists in three distinct persons: Father, Son, and Holy Spirit. There is one God, yet he is three persons; there are not three Gods, nor do the three persons merely represent different aspects or modes of a single divine being. While the term Trinity is not found in the Bible, the concept is repeatedly assumed and affirmed by the writers of Scripture (e.g., Matt. 28:19; Luke 1:35; 3:22; Gal. 4:6; 2 Thess. 2:13–14; Heb. 10:29).

[3] **Ascension** – The departure of the resurrected Jesus to God the Father in heaven (Luke 24:50–51; Acts 1:1–12).

WEEK 4: THE DEAD ALIVE BY GRACE

Ephesians 2:1–10

▲

The Place of the Passage

Believers' spiritual blessings come with access to the power of the sovereign ruler of the present and future ages. These blessings include riches that make earthly wealth pale in comparison. Such a lofty position could create a temptation to boast about these blessings or one's role in acquiring them. In Ephesians 2:1–10, Paul will abolish all cause for human boasting in salvation, leaving all the glory for salvation to God alone.

The Big Picture

God's merciful turning of the believers' depravity[1] into salvation through Christ glorifies the workmanship of God. The passage moves from a description of the depravity of all people to the working of God's mercy in Christ, concluding with a reminder of why our salvation is no cause for boasting.

> ### Reflection and Discussion

Read through the complete passage for this study, Ephesians 2:1–10. Then review the questions below concerning the way Paul describes salvation and write your notes on them. (For further background, see the *ESV Study Bible*, pages 2264–2265; available online at esv.org.)

1. Total Depravity (2:1–3)

"Dead" describes believers' moral and spiritual condition prior to salvation. Based on the description of this diagnosis in 2:1–3, what is the extent of this type of death?

Paul ties the Ephesians' pre-salvation behavior to the present world system. "The course of this world," "the prince of the power of the air," and "the spirit that is now at work in the sons of disobedience" are universal spiritual evils, the latter two referring to Satanic[2] activity. How do these terms add to our understanding of our spiritual status before we came to faith in Christ?

Paul will also relate the description "dead" to one's bodily passions. All people in the history of the world are included in this category ("all once lived"; "the rest of mankind"). According to Ephesians 2:3, how do unbelievers set goals and make decisions? Prior to Christ, what hope is there for the dead "sons of disobedience," whom Paul calls "children of wrath"?

2. Interception of Mercy (2:4–7)

Paul's sentence that spans these four verses places the main verb behind several modifying clauses. "Being rich in mercy," "because of the great love with which he loved us," and "even when we were dead in our trespasses" speak to God's character and motivation in salvation. How do the modifying terms embellish the contrast between 2:4 and 2:1–3? What does 2:4 say about the relationship between being "made alive" and the work of Christ in his earthly ministry?

Based on the contrast between 2:4 and 2:1–3, why would Paul conclude in 2:5 that he is describing a work of grace?

The description of salvation as raising and seating believers connects 2:5 to God's raising Christ from the dead and seating him at his right hand "in the heavenly places" (1:20). How does this connection magnify the working of grace in the process of salvation? In contrast to the eyes of people, what glory does this give to the church in the eyes of God?

Paul describes some of God's goals of salvation in "the coming ages." What do these goals indicate about the inheritance of believers?

---

3. A Beautiful Workmanship (2:8–10)

Paul now mentions "grace" for the third time in chapter 2, and for the sixth time in the letter (1:2, 6, 7; 2:5, 7, 8). He previously introduced the role of faith in salvation in 1:13, 15 and 19. How does the whole of Ephesians 2:1–8 help us see the relationship between grace and faith[3] in the believer's salvation?

Grammatically, "this is not of your own doing" refers to the entire clause containing "grace" and "faith." Both grace and faith come as gifts from God. Since faith is also a gift, what should believers conclude about their significance in their own salvation?

If salvation, including faith, "is not a result of works," how does this limit the boasting of the believer with respect to salvation?

The terms in 2:10 indicate that the "good works" of believers are wholly of God: believers are "his workmanship," things "prepared beforehand" by God and "created in Christ Jesus." What encouragement does this offer to Christian living—to the "walk" of believers, also mentioned in 4:1, 17; 5:2, 8, 15? In what ways does 2:10 reveal that the gospel must be an integral part of the daily walk of believers and of the ministry of the church?

Read through the following three sections on *Gospel Glimpses*, *Whole-Bible Connections*, and *Theological Soundings*. Then take time to consider the *Personal Implications* these sections may have for you.

Gospel Glimpses

THE SINFULNESS OF MAN. The starting place of Christian belief is our recognition that we are spiritually dead before God. This death entered mankind at the disobedience of Adam (Gen. 3:8; Hos. 6:7; Rom. 5:12). Although great humanitarian and philanthropic efforts often mask mankind's depravity, all people lack the spiritual and moral ability to please God. Instead of seeking after God, every man's natural inclination follows the working of Satan and base appetites that are contrary to God's will. Therefore, as Paul concludes in a metaphor of fatherly discipline, by nature all people stand in jeopardy of God's eternal wrath.

THE RICHNESS OF GRACE. God characterizes himself in one of his earliest covenantal revelations to the nation of Israel as "the LORD, the LORD, a God merciful and gracious" (Ex. 34:6). This revelation shines most brightly in the incarnation of Christ (John 1:16–17). God's grace in Christ stands between the believer and the wrath of God. Grace operates in the whole of salvation and all that attends it, including the faith of believers.

Whole-Bible Connections

THE WORLD, THE FLESH, THE DEVIL. Mankind is subject to the influence of three great enemies: the greater cultural worldview, one's natural desires and inclinations, and the Evil One (Gen. 3:1–7; 4:7, 23–24; 6:5; 11:4). All three work in harmony to keep mankind in happy disobedience to the Creator. As unbelievers, we seek the approval of other people, prefer our will to God's, and live as those deceived by Satan about sin and its penalty. These dispositions guide us toward greater personal and social destruction. Only the power of grace in Christ breaks into these arenas to bring a new view of the world, holy desires, and the truth.

Theological Soundings

UNION WITH CHRIST. Paul's head-body imagery inherently includes concepts of authority and submission. The imagery also manifests the mysterious union Christ has with his church. "In Christ" (Eph. 1:1, 3), "in him" (1:4, 7, 10, 11, 13), "through him" (1:5), "with Christ" (2:5), and other such terms elucidate the nature of this union. Christ is so united with believers that whatever he accomplished in salvation was accomplished in us; whatever he inherits as sovereign Lord, believers inherit with him. Through this union that began in election (1:4), the believer accomplishes work for God.

MONERGISM. The idea that God alone rescues sinners runs throughout this passage: 1) Unbelievers have no spark of spiritual life with which to search for God and find him; 2) God is the one who intervenes into a life dead in trespasses; 3) God makes the dead alive together with Christ; 4) grace saves and will be on display for all eternity; 5) grace and faith are gifts from God; and 6) we are the workmanship of God: "It is not of your own doing," notes the apostle. While Paul will call believers to walk before God toward maturity, even this must be God's doing. Therefore, it is right to speak of salvation—justification, sanctification, glorification, and more—as first to last a work of grace, even as believers act upon God's commands to do his will.

Personal Implications

Take time to reflect on the implications of Ephesians 2:1–10 for your own life today. Consider what you have learned that might lead you to praise God, repent of sin, and trust in his gracious promises. Make notes below on the personal implications for your walk with the Lord of the (1) *Gospel Glimpses*, (2) *Whole-Bible Connections*, (3) *Theological Soundings*, and (4) this passage as a whole.

1. Gospel Glimpses

2. Whole-Bible Connections

3. Theological Soundings

4. Ephesians 2:1–10

As You Finish This Unit . . .

Take a moment now to ask for the Lord's blessing and help as you continue in this study of Ephesians. And take a moment also to look back through this unit of study, to reflect on some key things that the Lord may be teaching you—and perhaps to highlight and underline these things to review again in the future. Think, too, of memorizing the key verse to the book: Ephesians 2:10.

Definitions

[1] **Depravity** – The sinful condition of human nature apart from grace, whereby humans are inclined to serve their own will and desires and to reject God's rule.

[2] **Satan** – A spiritual being whose name means "accuser." As a fallen angel and the leader of all the demonic forces, he opposes God's rule and seeks to harm God's people and accuse them of wrongdoing. His power, however, is confined to the bounds that God has set for him, and one day he will be destroyed along with all his demons (Matt. 25:41; Rev. 20:10).

[3] **Faith** – Trust in or reliance upon something or someone despite a lack of concrete proof. Salvation, which is purely a work of God's grace, can be received only through faith (Rom. 5:2; Eph. 2:8–9). The writer of Hebrews calls on believers to emulate those who have lived godly lives by faith (Hebrews 11).

WEEK 5: ONE NEW MAN

Ephesians 2:11–22

▲

The Place of the Passage

Ephesians 1 reveals that salvation consists of multiple blessings that began in eternity past to bring God glory through Christ. The blessings come to believers through their union with Christ, being experienced in the present life when one believes the gospel. Ephesians 2:1–10 explains that believers have no cause for boasting in the process, because they were wrath-bound sinners who had no inclination toward God; God alone interrupted the dead life with grace from Christ. In 2:11–22, Paul shows how this work of Christ creates one united identity among believers, foreshadowing the fullness of the union believers will share with God and one another for eternity.

The Big Picture

Ephesians 2:11–22 explains *reconciliation* and its implications for the common identity of Jewish[1] and Gentile believers in Christ for the present and future ages.

Reflection and Discussion

Read through the complete passage for this study, Ephesians 2:11–22. Then review the questions below concerning this section of Paul's letter to the church at Ephesus and write your notes on them. (For further background, see the *ESV Study Bible*, pages 2265–2266; available online at esv.org.)

1. Remembering Separation (2:11–13)

"Therefore" indicates that on the basis of God's gracious work (2:1–10), Paul is exhorting the Gentile believers in Ephesus to remember the depth of their separation from God. What is the significance of the references to Old Testament ideas like the "commonwealth of Israel" and "covenants of promise" in relation to the Gentiles' spiritual past? Why did the Gentiles' past identity as "the uncircumcision" render them hopeless before God?

b/c they did not have access to God and were seperate from his people (Israel)

In Christ's work of salvation, unbelieving Gentiles have been "brought near" to those who were circumcised "in the flesh by hands" (e.g., Israel). What, then, is one effect the death of Christ had on the ethnic relations of Jews and Gentiles? In what sense(s) were Gentiles "far off"? In what sense(s) are they now "near"?

They were seperated, different bodies of people and now they are the same to God and knit as a family

2. Christ Made Peace (2:14–18)

In 2:14, "in his flesh" is a reference to the death of Christ on the cross. By dying on the cross, Christ achieved peace[1] between Jews and Gentiles and so removed the source of their hostility with one another. What was the source of this hostility, and what does it mean for it to be abolished? In what sense are Jewish and Gentile believers "one new man"?

The dividing wall—the are no longer
commanded to be set apart and
all people have opportunity for relationship
with God through Christ. We all have
sin but it is covered by Christ – one
new man.

Christ proclaimed the message of peace to those "far off" and "those who were near" (2:17). What is the content of this message of peace? When did Christ preach to each of these groups in Ephesus?

Being "far from the commonwealth of Israel" rendered the Gentiles in need of the message of peace. Why did "those who were near" (Israel) also need this message of peace?

Romans 3:23
All need to be reconciled w/ God

As a result of the preaching of peace, what is new about the Jews' means of access to the Father? What is new about the Gentiles' access to the Father?

Jesus is the sacrifice and they no longer
have to abide by the ot law.
Gentiles have access for the first time.

3. The Church as God's Temple (2:19–22)

Christ's work of peace removes the believing Gentiles' status as "strangers and aliens." When Paul includes the Jewish believers in the new status of "no longer strangers and aliens," what does he reveal about the spiritual status of those who had the "covenants of promise"?

God fulfilled his covenant promises
through Christ who died for both
Jews & gentiles

The Ephesians' secular citizenship provided them with the responsibilities, rights, and benefits of the Roman city. Paul borrows this political language to describe the church as a new community formed by Christ—as a new citizenry and a new household. How does the language of 2:19 emphasize the corporate nature of this new community? What does such language intend to communicate about relationships between members of the body of Christ?

→ Strangers & aliens, citizens, members
Temple of God - Believers have become
the temple   his
"Where God meets people for joyful
   worship & fellowship"

What would Jewish and Gentile believers in Ephesus have understood about the gospel's effect on race relationships, nationalism, and individualism?

The cornerstone of a building was the stone ensuring a straight and stable foundation. How did the apostles and prophets act as the foundation for the church? What does Christ as cornerstone mean for the church?

They helped lay the foundation for the early church through their writings & preaching

Christ as cornerstone

"In him" repeats the theme of the believers' mysterious union with Christ. How does the Spirit's work in the temple fulfill the work of the head of this union, Christ (from 1:22)?

temple – own bodies & corporately
— spirit is growing us together
— Holy spirit is the guarantee of our inheritance (1:14)
— Spirit helps us fulfill the will of God

Read through the following three sections on *Gospel Glimpses*, *Whole-Bible Connections*, and *Theological Soundings*. Then take time to consider the *Personal Implications* these sections may have for you.

Gospel Glimpses

PEACE. Since the time of the fall, mankind's fellowship with the Creator has been broken. The sins of each individual continue the breaching of this relationship with a holy God. The reestablishment of the broken relationship depends upon one making an offering of peace and our own admitting to the brokenness of the relationship. On the cross, Christ sacrifices himself as the peace offering on behalf of mankind (Isa. 53:5). His death reconciles believers to God (Rom. 5:1). In him alone is the breach between each of us and the Creator repaired.

Whole-Bible Connections

GOD DWELLING AMONG HIS PEOPLE. In a world without sin, God dwelt among his people, and they enjoyed friendship and fellowship with one another (Gen. 3:8). After mankind's fall, Adam and Eve were banished from the garden and from God's immediate presence. Since then, the hope of God's people has been that God would again dwell among them. In the coming of Christ into the world, the hope of God's presence among his people is renewed as the "Word became flesh and dwelt among us" (John 1:14). Uniquely, in the person of Jesus Christ, God was dwelling among his people. All believers can personally experience God's dwelling among them through the person of the Holy Spirit (John 14:16–17).

THE LORD'S CORNERSTONE. The concept of a strategic cornerstone within the plan of God has ancient roots. One psalmist, possibly a Davidic king of Israel, identifies himself as the Lord's cornerstone, rejected by the nations but exalted by God (Ps. 118:22). Later, through the prophets the Lord speaks of laying a cornerstone in order to counter scoffers and poor leadership in Israel (Isa. 28:16; Zech. 10:4). Jesus interprets the cornerstone prophecies as references to himself and his ministry on behalf of Israel (Matt. 21:42; Mark 12:10; Acts 4:11). He is the rejected cornerstone that will be exalted above Israel's leaders and the nations through his death and resurrection. As such, he will crush those who oppose him (Luke 20:17–18; 1 Pet. 2:7–8).

Theological Soundings

NEW CREATION. The hope of the world is that God has promised a renewal of all things. This renewal includes a new heavens and earth (Isa. 65:17; Rev. 21:1). The renewal also has personal and present dimensions anticipating those cosmic dimensions. In salvation through Christ, God brings about a "new creation" in believers, giving them a new disposition—a desire to live lives pleasing to God and to crucify sinful desires (Rom. 6:4; 2 Cor. 5:17; Eph. 2:20–24; Col. 3:10). Corporately, believers express this newness as a redeemed humanity of loving and holy citizenship—as "one new man." This new man is the visible demonstration of the renewal Christ will make of the full creation (Rom. 8:23). Christ will lift the effects of the curse from the present world, even as he lifts the effects of the curse from individual believers.

> ## Personal Implications

Take time to reflect on the implications of Ephesians 2:11–22 for your own life today. Consider what you have learned that might lead you to praise God, repent of sin, and trust in his gracious promises. Make notes below on the personal implications for your walk with the Lord of the (1) *Gospel Glimpses*, (2) *Whole-Bible Connections*, (3) *Theological Soundings*, and (4) this passage as a whole.

1. Gospel Glimpses

2. Whole-Bible Connections

3. Theological Soundings

4. Ephesians 2:11–22

As You Finish This Unit . . .

Take a moment now to ask for the Lord's blessing and help as you continue in this study of Ephesians. And take a moment also to look back through this unit of study, to reflect on some key things that the Lord may be teaching you—and perhaps to highlight and underline these things to review again in the future.

Definitions

[1] **Jew** – A person belonging to one of the tribes of Israel. The term, derived from the word "Judah/Judean," came into being around the time of the Babylonian exile (c. 586 BC).

[2] **Peace** – In modern use, the absence of tension or conflict. In biblical use, a condition of well-being or wholeness that God grants his people, which also results in harmony with God and others.

WEEK 6: AN INTERLUDE ON THE MYSTERY OF GENTILE INCLUSION

Ephesians 3:1–13

The Place of the Passage

Ephesians 1–2 paints a grand picture of the Lord pouring his fullness into one new man to make a glorious temple. Now Paul intends to draw out practical implications of the church's identity in Christ for daily Christian life. However, he interrupts his direction to explain the relationship of the gospel to his imprisonment.

The Big Picture

In an excursus, Paul's revelation of the mystery of the Gentiles' equal inheritance in Christ is used to exhort the Ephesians to maintain strength of heart in spite of Paul's imprisonment for the gospel.

Reflection and Discussion

Read through Ephesians 3:1–13, the focus of this week's study. Following this, review the questions below and write your responses concerning this section of the book of Ephesians. (For further background, see the *ESV Study Bible*, pages 2266–2267; available online at esv.org.)

1. Revealing the Mystery (Eph. 3:1–6)

Ephesians 3:1 has wording very similar to 3:14 and 4:1 ("for this reason . . . for this reason . . . therefore"). Paul will resume his earlier line of thought in verse 14 after a significant digression concerning his calling as the apostle to the Gentiles. As a steward of God's grace, what responsibility does he have toward God and the Gentiles?

To bring the "mystery" to God's people and be a "minister" according to the gift of God's grace

"As I have written briefly" looks back to knowing the "mystery of his will" (1:9–10). In 3:3 Paul speaks of the "mystery made known . . . by revelation." How might speaking of the mystery in these terms encourage the Gentile believers in the congregation?

That Gentiles are fellow heirs, and part of Gods family with [those] access to Gods promises because of Christ and the Gospel.

Paul relates the mystery to the gospel by calling it the "mystery of Christ." In 3:5, what unique insights does Paul give concerning this mystery? Why would this have been important in helping the church understand the nature of Paul's imprisonment?

The suffering was on behalf of the Gentiles

After providing the background of his personal relationship to the mystery in 3:1–5, Paul finally reveals the content of the mystery in verse 6. How does the content of the mystery add knowledge about God's plan not previously revealed in the Old Testament or the Gospels? How does the mystery relate to the gospel?

Christ's death meant that all people now have access to God thru Christ the Gentiles are no co-heirs and recipients of God's promises

Based on the content of the mystery, why did Paul first provide several verses of background information?

To build credibility and to reveal the lengths he is called to go in communicating this message.

2. Encouraging the Church (3:7–13)

Paul views his stewardship as being a "minister according to the gift of God's grace" (v. 7). Yet Paul also views himself as the "very least of all the saints" (v. 8). Of what life event does Paul speak when he mentions the working of God's power? What does Paul's understanding of God's powerful grace say about his view of his imprisonment?

Acts 22: 17-21

Why would Paul use "the unsearchable riches of Christ" to describe his preaching to the Gentiles? When the church reads the phrase "hidden for ages in God who created all things," what does this add to their understanding about God's plan for Israel and the Gentiles?

we are never going to fully understand all the aspects but the Gentiles can rest that it was Gods plan.

Ps. 119
God speaking to who we will become

God's intent in Paul's preaching of the gospel is that the "manifold wisdom of God" would be made known through the church to the powers "in the heavenly places" (v. 10). Based on all that Paul has said so far in Ephesians, what is this "wisdom"? Why would the Lord intend the powers to see this wisdom?

In Christ, Paul and the church have "boldness and access with confidence" (v. 12). To what activity do these terms refer? How does this activity contribute to the church's encouragement as they hear of Paul's suffering on their behalf?

Read through the following three sections on *Gospel Glimpses, Whole-Bible Connections,* and *Theological Soundings.* Then take time to consider the *Personal Implications* these sections may have for you.

▶ Gospel Glimpses

BOLDNESS AND ACCESS. Believers do not live in a belief system governed by fate or by an inexorable cycle of history, for we have the ability to approach God and ask him to change us, those around us, and entire institutions. Through the cross, Jesus provides for his church the ability to approach God with confidence that he will hear our prayers and act with goodness according to his purposes and glory (Eph. 3:12; see Matt. 27:51; Heb. 4:14–18). The gospel gives us access to the one who controls history. Even in imprisonment, Paul took advantage of the privilege we have through Christ to approach the Creator as our loving Father.

SUFFERING FOR CHRIST. When believers live out their faith, they are certain to suffer persecution. Persecution for one may be living with a spouse hostile to the gospel; for another it might mean facing a mob intent on killing anyone who names the name of Christ. Just as our Lord suffered in his earthly ministry as he did the will of God, so too will believers be hated; the seed of the Serpent will remain in conflict with the seed of the woman (Gen. 3:15; Matt. 13:38; John 8:44; 15:18). The promise of suffering for the gospel, however, is not a reason to turn away from courageously and zealously proclaiming the gospel and serving in the most hostile regions of the world. Instead, like Paul, we should embrace the call to suffer with a view toward preaching the message of salvation to those who are lost, for the glory of Christ (1 Cor. 7:16; Eph. 3:7–11; Phil. 1:27–30). Such suffering is only temporary for those who have the promise of beholding the glory of God.

▶ Whole-Bible Connections

PLAN FOR THE GENTILES. In the Old Testament, God uniquely calls Israel among all peoples so that the nations might come to them to gain revelation about the true God (Deut. 7:6–8; Ps. 96:10; Isa. 49:6; 60:3). In contrast, Gentile nations appear as enemies of God and his people and as objects of divine judgment (Amos 1:2–15; Isaiah 17–21). It therefore might seem that the equal inclusion of the Gentiles in the inheritance of Christ comes only with the failure of Israel to reveal Christ to the nations. Yet Paul reveals that since eternity past, the plan of God always included Jews and Gentiles sharing in membership "of the same body" (Eph. 3:6). Neither Gentile inclusion in the church nor the church itself is an afterthought of God. Yet only in Christ have God's purposes been made known.

FULFILLMENT OF THE OLD TESTAMENT IN THE NEW. Augustine's dictum, "In the Old Testament the New Testament is concealed; in the New Testament the Old Testament is revealed," seeks to explain the relationship of the two Testaments to each other. The things the Lord intends to reveal or accomplish in the New Testament lie as seeds hidden in the Old Testament. The Old Testament reveals merely that the Lord will show mercy to the Gentiles through Israel (Gen. 18:18; 22:18; 26:14; 28:4; Isa. 11:10–12). The Old Testament revelation remains unfulfilled at the close of Malachi, anticipating new revelation. In the New Testament, the seeds of the Old Testament blossom into the flowers that become visible as one reads the Old Testament in light of Christ's redemption of his own. The plan of God for the Gentiles takes shape in the calling and establishment of the church (Acts 3:25; Rom. 9:25–26; Gal. 3:8).

Theological Soundings

MYSTERIES. The New Testament speaks of several mysteries—truths partially or completely concealed in the Old Testament that are unveiled in the New (Matt. 13:11; 1 Cor. 4:1). Paul reveals that the promise of God to dwell among his people finds fulfillment in Christ's residing in us through the indwelling Spirit (Col. 1:26–27). Through the resurrection of Christ, the hope of life beyond the grave is completed in the transformation of the believer's physical body (1 Cor. 15:51–53). Like the revelation of the mystery of the Gentiles' inheritance, each of these mysteries reveals a sovereign God working to accomplish his perfect will for the glory of Christ and the joy of God's people.

UNIVERSAL CALL. Paul's call to "bring [the gospel] to light for everyone" is also our calling. All are under the curse of sin and need the power of the death of Christ to break the curse (Rom. 3:23; 6:23; Gal. 3:10–14). The goal of the Great Commission is that people everywhere would hear the message of Christ. Yet it remains true that, in Christ, God elected before the world was created those who will be saved (Rom. 11:2–7; Eph. 1:4; 1 Pet. 1:1). The preaching of the gospel is a universal calling that brings about the salvation of the elect among Israel and the nations. This is the intent of Christ's words: "Many are called, but few are chosen" (Matt. 22:14).

> **Personal Implications**

Take time to reflect on the implications of Ephesians 3:1–13 for your own life today. Consider what you have learned that might lead you to praise God, repent of sin, and trust in his gracious promises. Make notes below on the personal implications for your walk with the Lord of the (1) *Gospel Glimpses*, (2) *Whole-Bible Connections*, (3) *Theological Soundings*, and (4) this passage as a whole.

1. Gospel Glimpses

2. Whole-Bible Connections

3. Theological Soundings

4. Ephesians 3:1–13

As You Finish This Unit . . .

Take a moment now to ask for the Lord's blessing and help as you continue in this study of Ephesians. Also take a moment to reflect on the Key Verse (2:10), and to look back through this unit of study in order to reflect on some key things that the Lord may be teaching you—and perhaps to highlight and underline these things to review again in the future.

Week 7: Prayer for Love

Ephesians 3:14–21

The Place of the Passage

Paul resumes his flow of thought, which had been interrupted by his discussion on the mystery of the Gentiles' inheritance of the promises of the gospel (compare "For this reason" [Eph. 3:14] to "For this reason" [3:1] and "therefore" [4:1]). He will offer a prayer as the conclusion of his explanation of the gospel implications for new citizenship and as the conclusion to Ephesians 1–3, where he has focused on the calling of the church, especially as it pertains to the Trinity (1:15–17; see also 4:1–6). His prayer will also serve as a transition to the practical outworking of the gospel in chapters 4–6.

The Big Picture

Reasoning from the need to persevere through persecution (Eph. 3:1–13), in Ephesians 3:14–21 Paul prays for the church to be strengthened by God's greatness. The prayer asks God to move the church to realize the significance of its singular identity as a body united in the Trinity.

> ## Reflection and Discussion

Read through the complete passage for this study, Ephesians 3:14–21. Then review the questions below concerning this pivotal section in the book of Ephesians and write your notes on them. (For further background, see the *ESV Study Bible*, page 2267; available online at esv.org.)

1. The Power of the Father and the Spirit (3:14–16)

Paul appropriately bows on his knees in humility before God the Father—the one who gives a measure of filial identity to all people on the earth. In what way are all people associated with the name of the Father? How does this naming relate to and magnify the new relationship of Jews and Gentiles that Paul revealed in 2:11–3:13?

For the fifth time Paul mentions the "riches" of grace found in Christ (compare Eph. 1:7, 8; 2:7; 3:8, 16). He asks the Father to give the church power from his riches. What is the nature of these riches? What is the relationship of the working of the Spirit to these riches (see also 1:14; 2:22)?

2. The Presence of Christ (3:17–19)

The immediate goal of Paul's prayer for the church is that "Christ may dwell in [their] hearts through faith" (3:17). The verses that follow clarify the working of the indwelling Christ. If Paul is speaking to believers, why does he ask for strength for Christ to dwell in them? What is the role of the believer's faith in this process?

Paul uses the idea of a tree being "rooted" to speak of the believers' lives. "Grounded" refers to the foundation of the believers as one body. What is Paul hoping the believers will *become*, if love does for them what soil does for a tree? What is he hoping they will *do* when they are grounded in love?

"Breadth and length and height and depth" express the great dimensions of the love of Christ (3:18). Why is strength from God needed to comprehend Christ's love? What would a lack of love within the church body have revealed about the Ephesian church?

"Filled with all the fullness of God" (3:19) points back to the "fullness of him who fills all in all" (1:23). By what measure could the Ephesians determine if their congregation was experiencing the fullness of God? How does this fullness relate to their identity with Christ in the present and the future, both spiritually and practically?

------

3. The Plan for the Church (3:20–21)

Paul concludes the first three chapters of Ephesians with a doxology.[1] How are "to him who is able to do far more than we can ask or think" fitting words of praise for what Paul has said in both 3:1–19 and, more generally, in all of Ephesians 1–3? What encouragement should the believers draw from the phrase "at work within us?"

What is Paul's final goal for the church of Ephesus in 3:21? What does this say about the hope of the gospel in each successive period of history?

Read through the following three sections on *Gospel Glimpses*, *Whole-Bible Connections*, and *Theological Soundings*. Then take time to consider the *Personal Implications* these sections may have for you.

Gospel Glimpses

THE GOSPEL AS LOVE. God's unselfish motivation in bringing many to glory is to achieve their highest good and thus express his own greatest passion and affection. Being in perfect and holy fellowship with the Son and the Spirit, it is love that moves the Father to bring the elect into his family as his children (Eph. 1:4–7). In Ephesians 2:4, Paul demonstrates that love compels God to bring sons of disobedience to salvation from wrath by mercy and grace. In 1 Corinthians 13, Paul will personify God's love for us as one who acts with patience, kindness, humility, consideration, joy, truth, endurance, hope, and faithfulness. It is these virtues that Paul desires the church to know with increasing depth, through the power of the Spirit. All of the church's acts, thoughts, motives, goals, and speech must sink their roots in love's soil, from there to draw nourishment for obedience and faithful gospel witness. Only Christ's love, flowing through every member, will show to wicked powers God's glorious wisdom in sending Christ.

Whole-Bible Connections

THE GLORY OF GOD. In the doxology at the end of Romans 11, Paul proclaims the glory of God as the goal of all things and all history (11:36). All things exist to make the Lord's greatness known, to display the beauty of his perfections, and to bring him the highest praise—praise above all things, including all earthly pursuits. When Moses asked the Lord to show him his glory, he understood this as the ultimate experience all creation seeks (Ex. 33:18). God revealed his glory in safe measures in the tabernacle and the temple (Ex. 40:34–35; 1 Kings 8:10–11). Peter, James, and John were given grace to behold Christ in his glory as Christ made God known to them in the transfiguration (Luke 9:28–32; John 1:14). Christ elects believers for "the praise of his glory" and intends to display this glory through the church in every generation of history and forever (Eph. 1:12, 14; 3:21).

PRAYING FOR THE CHURCH. Similar to the prayer in Ephesians 1:17–23, the prayer of Ephesians 3:14–21 asks for enlightenment, "that you . . . may have strength to comprehend" (3:18). In order for the church to have a grasp of God's glory corresponding to the greatness of Christ's salvation of the church, the Lord must provide spiritual insight. Seeing the fullness of the love of Christ in increasing measure requires greater illumination. Paul desires the Ephesians to experience the richness of a fuller understanding of Christ.

Theological Soundings

TRANSCENDENCE. From its opening pages the biblical story reveals God as a transcendent being. He existed before the creation as one distinct from the heavens and earth, calling all things into existence from nothing (Gen. 1:1–5). His "ways" and "thoughts" far exceed the thoughts of any finite, sinful being (Isa. 55:8–9). His greatness is so vast that it exceeds the ability of any earthly person to search out its depths (Ps. 145:3). As the great "I AM," *life itself* resides within him, in great contrast to those to whom he must *give* life and sustenance (Ex. 3:14; Acts 17:28; Col. 1:17; 1 Tim. 6:13; Heb. 1:4). Therefore, the measure of his love is greater than what a human mind can fully comprehend, and his ability to accomplish his will for the church far exceeds anything we could conceive of asking him to do (Eph. 3:19–20).

ETERNITY. "To him be glory in the church and in Christ Jesus throughout all generations, forever and ever" (Eph. 3:21). The Lord has existed from eternity past and will exist forever (Rev. 1:4, 8). His plan offers eternal life to those who believe on his Son (John 3:16). God's plan "in the fullness of time" (or "the coming ages") includes uniting all things in Christ (Eph. 1:10; 2:7). Each local body of believers has a stewardship over the gospel message and witness; all believers in Christ's body should keep an eternal perspective on all things so as to remember that everlasting life with God exceeds and influences all earthly pursuits.

Personal Implications

Take time to reflect on the implications of Ephesians 3:14–21 for your own life today. Consider what you have learned that might lead you to praise God, repent of sin, and trust in his gracious promises. Make notes below on the personal implications for your walk with the Lord of the (1) *Gospel Glimpses*, (2) *Whole-Bible Connections*, (3) *Theological Soundings*, and (4) this passage as a whole.

1. Gospel Glimpses

2. Whole-Bible Connections

3. Theological Soundings

4. Ephesians 3:14–21

As You Finish This Unit . . .

Take a moment now to ask for the Lord's blessing and help as you continue in this study of Ephesians. And take a moment also to look back through this unit of study, to reflect on some key things that the Lord may be teaching you—and perhaps to highlight and underline these things to review again in the future.

Definitions

[1] **Doxology** – Expression of praise to God. Often included at the end of NT letters. Modern church services often end with doxologies in the form of short hymns.

WEEK 8: CHRISTIAN MATURITY

Ephesians 4:1–16

The Place of the Passage

Paul will now exhort the Ephesians to consider the practical outworking of God's plan for the church. In Ephesians 1–3 he has exhibited the church as Christ's body—one new man created for good works that "God prepared beforehand, that we should *walk* in them" (2:10). In Ephesians 4–6 he develops the theme of "walking" as the new way of living for those in Christ (4:1, 17; 5:2, 8, 15).

The Big Picture

Paul's exhortation to the Ephesian believers to walk according to their calling recognizes the role of Christ's diverse gifts in the church's building itself up in love. Paul will move from an emphasis on the oneness of the members of the body to a focus on their works as individual members participating in the maturity of the local assembly.

Reflection and Discussion

Read the entire text for this week's study, Ephesians 4:1–16. Then review the following questions concerning this section of Ephesians and write your notes on them. (For further background, see the *ESV Study Bible*, pages 2267–2269; available online at esv.org.)

1. Trinitarian Unity (Eph. 4:1–6)

Paul urges the saints to walk "worthy of the calling to which you have been called, with all humility" (Eph. 4:1–2). How would you summarize this calling? Why are the virtues of humility, gentleness, and patience necessary to endure differences "in love" (v. 2) and to "maintain the unity" (v. 3) provided by the gospel?

Why does Christian unity necessitate agreement on "one body and one Spirit . . . one Lord, one faith, one baptism, one God and Father of all"? What might this say about the important interplay of doctrine[1] and unity? (Do Paul's words in vv. 4–6 remind you of a formal confession of faith, such as the Apostles' Creed?)

On the basis of Ephesians 4:1–6, what would walking *unworthy* of their calling have looked like among the Ephesian believers?

----

2. Gifted Diversity (Eph. 4:7–12)

"Grace was given to each one of us" (v. 7) indicates that every member of the body has a supernatural enabling that is important to a local congregation's fulfillment of its calling. Paul's quotation of Psalm 68:18 connects the giving of gifts to Christ's ascension. What is the significance of the ascension in empowering the church to fulfill the mandates of the gospel?

Jesus conquered demonic "captives" before ascending "far above all the heavens." Why did the descent of Christ "into the lower regions" need to precede his filling of all things?

Christ gave gifts to every believer through the outpouring of the Spirit. He also gave gifts to the corporate body of believers in this same outpouring, to "equip the saints for the work of ministry." In light of what Paul previously wrote (1:1; 2:20), how did the apostles' and prophets' ministries equip believers?

How do the ministries of evangelists, pastors, and teachers equip believers to do the work of building up the body? What attitudes should the Ephesians have toward the distinction between the roles of officers and members of the body?

----

3. Church Maturity (4:13–16)

Christ intends for his people to use their individual gifts to create an integrated body; he gives leaders so that each believer increases in the "knowledge of the Son of God." How does the proper functioning of gifts work to create unity among believers? What contributions do members of a church make toward helping one another mature in their understanding of Christ and his will for believers?

Once unity of the faith and knowledge of the Son of God is attained, the "one new man" (2:15) will reach full manhood—"the fullness of Christ." What does Paul say in 4:13–16 about the contribution of body life to the maturing of individual believers?

An assembly that grows is no longer "children," subject to deceptive teachings. How does a properly operating relationship between gifts, officers, unity, and knowledge of the Son help individual believers to live successfully in the church and the world?

How does "speaking the truth in love" (4:15) toward brothers and sisters facilitate growing up into the head of the body? If "every joint" and "each part" are working to bring about spiritual maturity in the church, how does Paul conclude that Christ, as the head, is accomplishing the growth of believers?

Read through the following three sections on *Gospel Glimpses*, *Whole-Bible Connections*, and *Theological Soundings*. Then take time to consider the *Personal Implications* these sections may have for you.

Gospel Glimpses

THE DESCENT OF CHRIST. "He descended into hell" is one line of the Apostles' Creed. While this line raises significant textual and theological questions, it seems to be reflective of two aspects of the redemptive work of Christ. First, Christ takes the penalty of hell upon himself as the wrath of God is poured out on him rather than on believers—as he becomes the propitiation for our sins (Rom. 3:25). Second, Christ does descend "into the lower regions" (Eph. 4:9) in order to defeat death and to triumph over the demonic (Col. 2:15). (See the *ESV Study Bible*, page 2268.)

GIFTS TO THE CHURCH. In the ascension, Christ returned from the earth to his throne as vice-regent in heaven (Eph. 4:8). From there he sent the Holy Spirit into the world to empower believers for the task of gospel proclamation (Acts 1:4, 8; 2:33–35). With the coming of the Spirit also came gifts to the church so that believers might have supernatural resources for serving Christ in the world. Paul's writings reveal special gifts given to leaders of the church to equip believers to build themselves up in Christ (4:11–12). We also read of individual gifts given to every believer (Rom. 12:3–8; 1 Cor. 12:4–11). The resurrection and exaltation of Christ continue to benefit the church with practical empowerment to edify itself in love.

Whole-Bible Connections

PASTORS.[2] The ongoing care of church membership falls to elders—qualified men who humbly shepherd believers according to the Word of God (Acts 14:23; 20:28; 1 Tim. 5:17–22; Titus 1:5; 1 Pet. 5:2–5). Traditionally in the church, among the elders is the office of pastor, a vocational servant who gives primacy to preaching and teaching for equipping believers for service to one another (Eph. 4:11–12; 1 Tim. 3:1). The office of pastor follows the train of the shepherds of Israel, who were to lead the people according to the law of God. Unfortunately, many of Israel's shepherds failed their callings, instead taking advantage of the flock (Ezekiel 34). God promised to replace their shepherds so that he himself might shepherd his people in righteousness (Ezek. 34:15). Christ has come as that Good Shepherd—the Great Shepherd who cares for all of the Lord's sheep (Gen. 49:24; John 10:1–18; 1 Pet. 2:25). To him, shepherds of local congregations look for the model and for final accountability as their Chief Shepherd (1 Pet. 5:4). Each believer and every congregation increases their own blessings when they submit themselves in obedience to Christlike pastors and elders (Heb. 13:17).

Theological Soundings

CHRIST-FILLED UNIVERSE. The consummation of history will include the awesome, sinless, perfect uniting of believers with God and with one another, such that we will be in him and he in us (Eph. 1:22–23; 1 Pet. 2:5), he will be one with the Father and the Spirit (John 10:28–30; 17:11, 22), and we will be members of one another (Eph. 2:19; 5:30). Then he who fills all in all will give all glory and honor to God the Father so that the Father might be all and in all (1 Cor. 15:24–28; Eph. 1:10, 23; 4:10). The glory and joy of this experience for believers will be beyond anything we can describe or imagine (1 Cor. 2:9).

BIBLICAL COMMUNITY. The church of Christ begins in the eternal election of believers in mercy as God's workmanship; it does not have its origin in a social theory of people who decide they want to start a new assembly (Eph. 1:3–6; 2:4, 10). This chosen community may express itself in local congregations, but it is Christ's church only to the extent that it is reflective of the calling, building, structuring, and governing of the church as Christ purposes and prescribes. This includes members, empowered by the Spirit of God and working in humility and unity under their leaders, lovingly building up one another toward maturity in Christ (Rom. 12:10; Gal. 6:2; 1 Thess. 3:2; Heb. 10:24).

Personal Implications

Take time to reflect on the implications of Ephesians 4:1–16 for your own life today. Consider what you have learned that might lead you to praise God, repent of sin, and trust in his gracious promises. Make notes below on the personal implications for your walk with the Lord of the (1) *Gospel Glimpses*, (2) *Whole-Bible Connections*, (3) *Theological Soundings*, and (4) this passage as a whole.

1. Gospel Glimpses

2. Whole-Bible Connections

3. Theological Soundings

4. Ephesians 4:1–16

As You Finish This Unit . . .

Take a moment now to ask for the Lord's blessing and help as you continue in this study of Ephesians. And take a moment also to look back through this unit of study, to reflect on some key things that the Lord may be teaching you—and perhaps to highlight and underline these things to review again in the future. Review your Key Verse.

Definitions

[1] **Doctrine** – A body of beliefs or teachings, often in systematic form.

[2] **Pastor** – A common translation of the Greek for "shepherd," which came to be used of leaders of the church, who are to "shepherd" the "flock" of believers in Christ.

Gospel verses to memorize:
Eph 4:32

WEEK 9: WALKING IN A NEW LIFE

Ephesians 4:17–32

▲

The Place of the Passage

In Ephesians 4:1–16, Paul focused on the believer's growth within a local congregation—with "one another" (v. 2) in "the whole body" (v. 16). Paul turns now to the believer's growth in dealings among "the Gentiles" (v. 17)—outside the church in wider society. Reminiscent of the discussion in 2:1–10 of the change from depravity to salvation, 4:17–32 shows that life in Christ demands a radical change in one's behavior. The change distances the believer's character from behavior acceptable to those hostile to Christ.

The Big Picture

The believer's new life in Christ leaves the practices of the old life and takes on the character and practices of Christ. Paul portrays the Ephesians' former Gentile ways as acts of ignorance. The Christian life will raise the bar on civility and morality.

Reflection and Discussion

Read through the complete text for this study, Ephesians 4:17–32. Then review the questions below concerning this important passage of Ephesians and write your notes on them. (For further background, see the *ESV Study Bible*, pages 2269–2270; available online at esv.org.)

1. Ignorance as Gentiles (4:17–19)

Paul will "testify in the Lord" against believers who are living like unbelieving Gentiles. What tone does this give to the coming discussion? Why is this tone important for the exhortation that follows?

Paul diagnoses the Gentiles' futility as atheistic ignorance (4:18) and amoral behavior according to "every kind of impurity" (v. 19). How then should the Ephesian Christians have evaluated the common and accepted worldviews and moral standards of the Gentiles?

----

2. Renewal in God (4:20–24)

"But that is not the way you learned Christ!" In 4:20–21, Paul draws a sharp line between the believers' former manner of living and the new life found in Christ. How important are correct hearing of the gospel and faithful discipleship to shedding the old life and taking on the new way of living? What connection does Paul make between sound doctrine and sanctification[1]?

Paul will develop the distinction between the "old self" and the "new self" in 4:25–32. What initial contrasts does he make between the old and new manners of life in 4:22–24? How does "renewed" thinking affect the unclothing of the old self? Why is renewed thinking needed to make clothing oneself in Christ effective?

3. Reflection of Christ (4:25–32)

Paul gives several imperatives for practical contrasts that should distinguish a believer's new manner of life from the old. Broadly speaking, the morality of the believer will go beyond common altruism and the standards of the Mosaic law[2] because of the new law found in Christ. Why does a believer's new membership require a renewed thinking about truth in personal relationships? What does the phrase "members of one another" suggest about the motives behind the falsehood that controls the Gentiles' lifestyle?

The believer has a renewed outlook on anger. Not every expression of anger is acceptable. There are both righteous and corrupt forms of anger. How might a believer fall prey to sin while displaying anger? How does quickly resolving anger show the likeness of God? In what ways does a wrong handling of anger allow an "opportunity" for the Devil in the life of a believer?

Renewed thinking also influences the work ethic and speech of a believer. What newness does the power of Christ bring to the Ephesians' work habits? What must be "put off" and "put on" in the believer's speaking? What unique elements of Christian speech display the gospel's working in a believer?

Why is the Holy Spirit's work in sealing a believer significant to that believer's renewed speech? (See also 1:13–14).

What message might removal of "all bitterness and . . . all malice" give to non-believers around us? How would the removal of slander and personal malice work to the benefit of each believer within a congregation?

The Christian virtues named in 4:32 anticipate the occurrences of disagreements both within and outside the assembly. What might kindness, tenderheartedness, and forgiveness have looked like during and/or in the aftermath of a conflict in the church in Ephesus? How does reflection on the forgiveness found in Christ contribute to peace among believers and a powerful witness in society at large?

Read through the following three sections on *Gospel Glimpses*, *Whole-Bible Connections*, and *Theological Soundings*. Then take time to consider the *Personal Implications* these sections may have for you.

Gospel Glimpses

IGNORANCE OF GOD. The Lord's holiness hides him from the eyes of unbelievers. While his work as creator is visible and tangible to all people (Ps. 19:1–3), unrighteousness moves us to disregard what we see and feel. Lack of knowledge of the one true God renders mankind susceptible to God's judgment. Only the proclamation of the truth of Christ in the gospel removes ignorance about God and makes possible experience of the gospel as the power of God for salvation (Rom. 1:16–17).

NEW LIFE. A popular and unfortunate teaching in some Christian communities creates two categories of sanctification among believers: "mature" and "carnal" Christians. Carnal believers would be those who profess salvation but lack any discernable sign of a changed life. In contrast to that teaching, Paul portrays a marked contrast between the new and former manners of life in a believer transformed by the spiritual blessings given in Christ. Christ's power so overcomes those in whom he lives that they increasingly exhibit godly traits such as trustworthiness, proper handling of anger, a healthy perspective on work, mature use of language, and a wealth of resources for addressing conflict. We don't achieve perfection in this life, but as we are continually renewed in Christ, increasingly we take on the image of God and his holiness.

> ## Whole-Bible Connections

SHARING WITH THE POOR. Caring for the poor has been a hallmark of God's people throughout history. Israel was taught not to charge her poor members interest on loans and to protect them from prejudiced perversions of justice in lawsuits (Ex. 22:25; 23:3, 6). The law made provision for the poor to eat at the expense of those with means and to maintain their meager goods with dignity (Ex. 23:11; Lev. 19:10; 23:22; 25:36, 39; Deut. 24:12–15). Remembering the Lord's kindness toward their spiritual poverty, the sons of Jacob kindly returned kindness toward those in physical poverty (Prov. 14:31; 19:17). The early church collected funds to provide supplies for believers facing poverty (Acts 11:27–30; Rom. 15:25–26; Gal. 2:10; 1 Cor. 16:1–3). Christ's atoning work graciously directs the use of a believer's financial resources to help the poor (Eph. 4:28).

TRUTHFULNESS. Many people think of deception in their personal and business transactions as acceptable as long as they are not caught. The shock from news stories about shady and unscrupulous practices dissipates quickly as further cases of deception arise. Being a person of complete truth, however, is one of the great changes Christ produces in his people (Eph. 4:21, 25).

> ## Theological Soundings

THE DEVIL. "Give no opportunity to the devil" (Eph. 4:27). The great enemy of God and Christians looks for occasions to bring about spiritual failure in God's people (1 Pet. 5:8). It is part of his chosen work to destroy the ministry of Christ in the church's proclamation of the gospel so that people will not believe (Luke 8:12). The Devil was bold enough to tempt the Lord to sin (Matt. 4:1; Luke 4:13); he constantly tempts believers toward pride (1 Tim. 3:6–7). His power is great enough to oppress people physically and even incite murder (John 8:44; Acts 10:38). A believer's only recourse against this powerful foe is the might of Christ (6:10–20). In Christ alone will believers find strength to resist the Devil and make him flee (James 4:7). He is a formidable opponent of the believer, and his reality should not be minimized or dismissed. Yet he is no match for God, who created him. His future destruction is certain (Matt. 25:41; 1 John 3:8; Rev. 20:10). As Martin Luther wrote, "One little word shall fell him."

> ## Personal Implications

Take time to reflect on the implications of Ephesians 4:17–32 for your own life today. Consider what you have learned that might lead you to praise God, repent

of sin, and trust in his gracious promises. Make notes below on the personal implications for your walk with the Lord of the (1) *Gospel Glimpses*, (2) *Whole-Bible
Connections*, (3) *Theological Soundings*, and (4) this passage as a whole.

1. Gospel Glimpses

2. Whole-Bible Connections

3. Theological Soundings

4. Ephesians 4:17–32

As You Finish This Unit . . .

Take a moment now to ask for the Lord's blessing and help as you continue in this study of Ephesians. And take a moment also to look back through this unit of study, to reflect on some key things that the Lord may be teaching you—and perhaps to highlight and underline these things to review again in the future.

Definitions

[1] **Sanctification** – The process of being conformed to the image of Jesus Christ through the work of the Holy Spirit. This process begins immediately after regeneration and continues throughout a Christian's life.

[2] **Law** – When spelled with an initial capital letter, "Law" refers to the first five books of the Bible (the *Pentateuch*). The Law contains numerous commands of God to his people, including the Ten Commandments and instructions regarding worship, sacrifice, and life in Israel. The NT often uses "the law" (lower case) to refer to the entire body of precepts set forth in the books of the Law.

WEEK 10: WALKING IN LOVE

Ephesians 5:1–14

The Place of the Passage

Paul continues to expound on the new life that results from the outworking of Christ's election of the believer. As head of the church, Christ's power transforms the body so that believers' behavior is vastly different from the natural ways practiced in the world. Some of the strongest warnings against sin and most graphic descriptions of sin and judgment in all of Paul's writings are found in this passage.

The Big Picture

In Ephesians 5:1–14, the believer's walk of love imitates Christ in order to please God and avoid the dangers of the works of darkness. The passage begins by presenting an ethical basis for the call away from worldly vices. The remainder of the verses toggles between spiritually dark vices and the consequences of continuing in them.

Reflection and Discussion

Read through the complete passage for this study, Ephesians 5:1–14. Then review the questions below and record your notes and reflections on this section of Ephesians. (For further background, see the *ESV Study Bible*, page 2270; available online at esv.org.)

1. New Role Model (5:1–6)

Paul calls the believers to be "imitators of God" just as children imitate the behavior of their parents. How does the parent-child relationship that God shares with us raise the level of expectation of a changed life? How does imitating one who was a "fragrant offering" strengthen the motivation for believers to imitate Christ?

Paul's prohibitions against ungodly passions are absolute—they "must not even be named among you." Based on 5:1–2 (and all of Ephesians 1–4), why is it "proper among saints" to separate completely from the vices of sexual immorality, impurity, and covetousness[1]?

Why are indecent behavior ("filthiness"), words of foolishness, and crude joking "out of place" for the children of God? How does thanksgiving work in the heart and mind of the believer to counter the believer's attraction to these three vices?

Paul places covetousness within the realm of "idolatry."[2] How is Paul able to equate them?

In what sense does Paul exclude from inheritance in the kingdom of God[3] believers who fall into sexual immorality, make themselves impure, or covet the possessions of others? What impetus for imitating Christ does this add to the call to walk in love?

Paul warns the Ephesians against "empty words" that could tempt them to forfeit the inheritance promised to believers. To what sort of words might Paul be referring? How does the reference to God's wrath help clarify the warning about missing the inheritance promised to believers?

2. New Partnerships (5:7–14)

When Paul says, "Do not become partners with them" (v. 7), he places limitations on the relationships of believers to the surrounding culture. Based on the previous use of "at one time . . . but now" in 2:11–13, what does Paul mean by this metaphorical use of "darkness" and "light"? What is Paul saying about the significance of one's salvation in making decisions about types of relationships one should develop or maintain with the "sons of disobedience"?

As the "fruit of light," how does the child of God walk as a child "of light"? How does walking as a child of light help one live pleasingly before God?

The vices Paul prohibits are "unfruitful" before God. How does walking as a child of light make it evident to unbelievers that their lack of morality needs to be exposed?

How does Paul's use of "light" in Ephesians 5:13 clarify what he means by "expose"? To what is Paul referring in the process of going from being exposed (v. 13) to becoming light (v. 14)?

The quotation in 5:14 might represent a mixture of lines from Isaiah 9:2; 26:19; 50:9–10; and 60:1–2. Based on Paul's use of light and darkness, when the "sleeper" awakes, what will be taking place in his life?

Read through the following three sections on *Gospel Glimpses*, *Whole-Bible Connections*, and *Theological Soundings*. Then take time to consider the *Personal Implications* these sections may have for you.

Gospel Glimpses

PLEASING AROMA. Scripture records Noah making the first offering described as a "pleasing aroma" (Gen. 8:21). Noah sheds the blood of several clean animals and offers them as burnt offerings. The fragrance from the offering—indicating an atoning sacrifice—sufficiently satisfies God's displeasure against man's evil to prevent another flood judgment. The various offerings of the law provide this same pleasing aroma (Ex. 29:18, 25, 41; Lev. 1:9, 13, 17). The goal of these offerings is to make sinful people pleasing to God. And, despite the failure of Israel to follow the Lord in obedience, the Lord nevertheless promises to make them a pleasing aroma (Ezek. 20:41). Redemptive history reveals Christ to be the fulfillment of the fragrant offering and acceptable sacrifice that provides the pleasing aroma to God, making sinful people pleasing in his sight (Heb. 7:27; 9:14; 10:12).

SUBSTITUTION. From the time of the fall, substitutionary sacrifice has been the God-given hope of mankind. Since we humans cannot pay the penalty for our sin, a substitute is needed (Rom. 6:23). Therefore, God promises a "seed" who will come and take the bruising that should be man's (Gen. 3:15). The slaying of animals to provide skins to cover Adam and Eve's guilt and take away their insufficient covering for sin provides an early foreshadowing of Christ's substitution for us (Gen. 3:21). Similarly, God's provision of a ram in place of Isaac (Gen. 22:8, 13) and a slain goat for Israel's sin (Lev. 16:7–10, 20–22) each point forward to the Lamb of God (John 1:36). Christ is the just one who gave himself for the unjust, the one without sin who became sin for us (2 Cor. 5:21; Eph. 5:2; 1 Pet. 3:18).

Whole-Bible Connections

COVETOUSNESS. Covetousness of any kind runs contrary to the gospel. The law of God establishes coveting as sin (Ex. 20:17; Deut. 5:21). Coveting reveals a heart unsatisfied with God's provision. This sin has plagued mankind throughout its history, arising first in Eve (Gen. 3:6; Rom. 1:29). The believer must fight covetousness at every turn (Luke 12:15; Eph. 5:3; Col. 3:5). So powerful is this sin even among believers that it often sits at the root of conflict within the church (James 4:1–5).

LIGHT VERSUS DARKNESS. When the earth was formless and void, and no physical light was present in the universe, God called light out of darkness (Gen. 1:3; 2 Cor. 4:6). Since that time, "light" and "darkness" have stood for the metaphorical polar opposites of righteousness and evil. The plague of darkness over Egypt was indicative of their spiritual darkness, whereas the light among the Israelites indicated their beloved status before God (Ex. 10:22–23). Gentiles walking in darkness were to see a great light in the coming of Christ (Isa. 9:1–2; Matt. 4:16–17). Eventually, the one who came as the Light of the World hung on a cross in darkness, bearing the reproach of sinners (Matt. 27:45; Mark 15:33; Luke 23:44). Believers cannot walk in darkness while claiming to have fellowship with God; instead, they must "walk in the light, as [God] is in the light" (1 John 1:6–7).

Theological Soundings

INHERITANCE OF THE KINGDOM OF GOD. Three times in Paul's writings he excludes sinful people from the kingdom of God (1 Cor. 6:9–10; Gal. 5:21; Eph. 5:5). These references to the destiny of unbelievers serve as strong warnings to believers to examine themselves for evidence of a life transformed by

Christ. The warnings do not question the salvation of those called by God. Instead, they recognize that believers do not live in sin, and that people who choose to live in sin should not deceive themselves by thinking they are believers.

SEXUAL IMMORALITY. Ephesians 5:1–5 condemns sexual immorality as behavior that does not flow from love (vv. 1–2), is not self-sacrificing (v. 2), does not imitate Christ (v. 2), is improper for saints (v. 3), and excludes participation in the inheritance of the kingdom of Christ. Paul calls for sexual purity in the life of the believer—possible only by the power of Christ (4:22–24). The apostle does not portray sexual immorality as something one cannot overcome or resist. Instead, Paul's writings consistently demand that sexual immorality become a thing of the past, in accord with the new life that comes in Christ (1 Cor. 5:9–11; 6:9–11; 10:8; Gal. 5:19; Col. 5:3; 1 Thess. 4:3; 1 Tim. 1:10).

Personal Implications

Take time to reflect on the implications of Ephesians 5:1–14 for your own life today. Consider what you have learned that might lead you to praise God, repent of sin, and trust in his gracious promises. Make notes below on the personal implications for your walk with the Lord of the (1) *Gospel Glimpses*, (2) *Whole-Bible Connections*, (3) *Theological Soundings*, and (4) this passage as a whole.

1. Gospel Glimpses

2. Whole-Bible Connections

3. Theological Soundings

4. Ephesians 5:1–14

> ### As You Finish This Unit . . .

Take a moment now to ask for the Lord's blessing and help as you continue in this study of Ephesians. And take a moment also to look back through this unit of study, to reflect on some key things that the Lord may be teaching you—and perhaps to highlight and underline these things to review again in the future.

Definitions

[1] **Covetousness** – The desire to have something (or someone) that belongs to another. Covetousness is forbidden in the Ten Commandments (Ex. 20:17; Deut. 5:21).

[2] **Idolatry** – In the Bible, often refers to the worship of a physical object. Paul's comments in Colossians 3:5 suggest that idolatry can include covetousness, since it is essentially equivalent to worshiping material things.

[3] **Kingdom of God/heaven** – The sovereign rule of God. At the present time, the fallen, sinful world does not belong to the kingdom of God, since it does not submit to God's rule. Instead, God's kingdom can be found in heaven and among his people (Matt. 6:9–10; Luke 17:20–21). After Christ returns, however, the kingdoms of the world will become the kingdom of God (Rev. 11:15). Then all people will, either willingly or regretfully, acknowledge his sovereignty (Phil. 2:9–11). Even the natural world will be transformed to operate in perfect harmony with God (Rom. 8:19–23).

WEEK 11: WALKING IN THE SPIRIT

Ephesians 5:15–6:9

The Place of the Passage

After exhorting the Ephesians to embrace general Christian virtues and warning them against general worldly vices, Paul now provides instructions for living out the calling of Christ within the spheres of home and work. The command to be filled with the Spirit joins the command to walk wisely, indicating that the believer needs Spirit-filled wisdom, in addition to Spirit-wrought power for love and submission, to carry out these commands. Recurring themes related to the gospel and the will of God in these verses accent the entire theological thrust of Ephesians.

The Big Picture

Ephesians 5:15–6:9 calls believers to Christlike actions in marriage, parenting, and work habits. Each set of instructions will make multiple appeals to the person and work of "the Lord"/"Christ," looking back to the one who has blessed the Ephesians with every spiritual blessing (5:22, 23, 25, 29; 6:1, 4, 5, 6, 9). The worship wrought by the filling of the Spirit begins the discussion as the necessary means of carrying out these instructions, which are often referred to as Paul's "household code."

> ## Reflection and Discussion

Read through Ephesians 5:15–6:9, the passage for this week's study. Then review the following questions, taking notes on this significant contribution to Ephesians' full message. (For further background, see the *ESV Study Bible*, pages 2271–2273; available online at esv.org.)

1. Wisdom and Filling for Worship and Submission (Eph. 5:15–21)

The final "walk" command contrasts wise ways of living with foolish decisions (5:15). In this context, why does Paul call for discernment by believers concerning their use of time? In contrast to living unwisely and foolishly, how does a believer discern the "will of the Lord"?

Paul juxtaposes "drunk with wine" with "filled with the Spirit" (5:18). What sort of differences characterize one who enjoys debauchery and one whose life gives evidence of being full of the Spirit? Why might each of the acts of a Spirit-filled life make the Ephesians' gospel proclamation appealing to those living as pagans?

With what corporate actions would the Ephesians have followed the instruction, "addressing *one another* in psalms and hymns and spiritual songs"?

2. Wisdom-Filled Marriage (Eph. 5:22–33)

Paul brings wisdom, and the submission of one filled with the Spirit, to the discussion of Christian marriage. It is evident from the pattern in 5:22–6:9 that those in subordinate roles practice submission—i.e., wives submit to husbands (5:22), children obey parents (6:1), bondservants obey masters (6:5)—and not vice versa. Those in authority act in wisdom toward their subordinates, i.e., husbands love sacrificially (5:25), fathers avoid provoking their children to anger (6:4), masters treat their slaves fairly (6:9). Why does a wife's submissive character bring glory to Christ in the world? Based on the analogy of Christ, what is the scope of the authority granted to a husband in a Christian marriage?

Paul calls husbands to a love of their wives shaped profoundly by Christ's work for the church on the cross—he "gave himself up for her" (5:25). What was Christ's goal for the church when he died in her place (vv. 26–27)? How, then, might the commands given to the Christian husband make greater demands than the commands given to the Christian wife?

How should the body analogies of a man's self-care and Christ's work for the church inform the husband's practice of love toward his wife?

Paul teaches that the original institution of marriage spoke about Christ and the church as a mystery (Gen. 2:24; Eph. 5:32). If the analogy concerns Christ's *incarnation* ("leave his father") and *death* ("hold fast to his wife"), to what does "the two shall become one flesh" correspond? Why does the analogy require "love" and "respect" from a husband and wife in a Christian marriage?

3. Wisdom-Filled Children and Parents (6:1–4)

Christ should transform the behavior of a redeemed child and a redeemed father of believing children. On what basis can Paul make the blanket judgment "for this is right" when instructing children to obey parents "in the Lord" (6:1)? What common social factors would prompt Paul to use the promise of Exodus 20:12, "that your days may be long in the land," to motivate a child to obedience?

Why is it important for a Christian father to avoid provoking his children to anger? How does one faithfully educate a child Christianly in the home? What might the instruction to fathers say about the necessity of dependence on the Holy Spirit?

4. Wisdom-Filled Slaves and Masters (6:5–9)

In Roman culture, a bondservant could own his own property; but even so, he may have had limited rights under his master and could have become the object of abuse. Yet one should not think of contemporary forms of racially driven slavery, kidnapping of children to make soldiers, or sex trafficking when thinking of the bondservants mentioned in the Bible, for they are not equivalent. A better modern-day comparison would be an employee under the authority of a supervisor, manager, or owner. In 6:5–8, Paul adds eight modifying clauses to the command for slaves to obey. How would obeying masters to the extent of each modifying clause have worked to transform and dismantle slavery in Ephesus?

What significance would God's rewarding bondservants and freemen equally (6:8) give to the obedience of the bondservant to his earthly master?

Why is threatening one employed as a bondservant contrary to the gospel? How might knowledge of an impartial Master in heaven guide a Christian employer's treatment of his employees (6:9)?

Read through the following three sections on *Gospel Glimpses, Whole-Bible Connections*, and *Theological Soundings*. Then take time to consider the *Personal Implications* these sections may have for you.

Gospel Glimpses

SANCTIFICATION. Those made morally unclean by sin may not approach God. Yet all persons in this world are stained by sin, and believers still sin even after their justification in Christ. Christ, however, is actively purifying his bride from all remaining sin (Eph. 5:26). In his death, Christ provided the cleansing that gives the believer a new status before God. In his present rule, Christ faithfully works to set the believer apart from sin for holiness until the entire church comes before him as a bride adorned in perfect beauty (v. 27).

Whole-Bible Connections

COSMIC MARRIAGE. There is mystery associated with marriage—the mystery of the gospel. In the history of salvation,[1] the initial relationship God establishes between Adam and Eve is that of marriage (Gen. 2:24; Matt. 19:4–5). God identifies Israel as his wife on the basis of their covenantal relationship (Hos. 2:2, 16, 19). Yet Israel is found guilty of adultery as she seeks after idols (Ex. 34:15; Jer. 2:35–36; Hos. 3:1). This cosmic marriage experiences divorce as the wife's worship turns to other lovers (Isa. 50:1; Jer. 3:8; Hos. 2:2). The Lord alone makes provisions to receive back his wife (Hos. 1:10–11; 2:14–15). In calling the church his bride, Christ intends for earthly marriage to display the hope of the heavenly marriage (Eph. 5:23, 27, 31–32). When the people of God are glorified, we all will enjoy marriage to Christ, rejoice in the marriage supper of the Lamb (Rev. 19:7, 9), and enjoy the consummation of the eternal marriage forever and ever (Rev. 21:1–4).

CORPORATE SINGING. Israel first sings together as one people immediately after deliverance from Egypt and God's defeat of their enemies (Exodus 15). The call to congregational singing is strong in the psalms (Pss. 21:13; 30:4; 33:3; 47:6–7; 95:1). Psalm singers exhort the people of the nations, too, to sing to the Lord in anticipation of his salvation of all nations (Pss. 66:4; 67:4; 68:32; 96:1; 98:4). Corporate singing is the act of a people excited about, and grateful for, their Savior and Redeemer (Isa. 26:19; 44:23; 49:13; 52:8; Jer. 31:12; Zech. 2:10). It is a simple yet heartfelt way for the united corporate body of God's people to exalt him with praise and thanksgiving for his mighty acts in creation and salvation. On this side of the cross, Paul encourages congregational singing as both a result of being filled with the Spirit and a means of deepening a congregation in the wisdom of the Word of God as the members sing to "one another"

(Eph. 5:19; Col. 3:16). The apostle places emphasis on the heart of the believer before Christ regardless of the style of song (Eph. 5:19; Col. 3:17). Singing congregationally will be the church's experience for all of eternity as we are enveloped in the glory and love of God forever (Zeph. 3:17; Rev. 5:9; 14:3; 15:3).

Theological Soundings

SLAVERY. Slavery is one of the oldest institutions of man. While some cultures have practiced slavery as a means of helping the poor or employing skilled workers (Ex. 21:1–6; Deut. 15:12–18), many cultures use slavery as a means to separate and subjugate a class or race of people, while exalting the owners and making them wealthy. Paul's instructions on slavery and the slave-master relationship are complex. Although he never calls for dismantling the institution, he does encourage Christian slaves to gain their freedom when possible (1 Cor. 7:21). However, those who remain slaves to human masters should see themselves as free in Christ (1 Cor. 7:22). Peter would later add that slaves should submit themselves even to masters who treat them cruelly or unjustly, following the example of Christ (1 Pet. 2:18–25). The godly actions of believing slaves and masters manifest the life-changing power of Christ to all (Titus 2:9), make the slaves better employees (Eph. 6:6–7), promote brotherhood and equality in Christ between slave and master (v. 9; Philem. 15–16), and give dignity to all slaves as Christian masters deal kindly with those under their authority (Eph. 6:9). The fact that slavery in the modern world is not practiced with any sense of Christian ideals, but instead degrades, abuses, tortures, and dehumanizes people as captives, sex objects, or property, argues for the Christian to seek the abolition of slavery today as an act of justice (Ps. 82:4; Prov. 21:3, 15; 24:10–12; Isa. 58:6–7; Mic. 6:8; Matt. 12:18–20; Luke 11:42).

THANKSGIVING. Giving thanks to the Lord from the heart is a result of being full of the Spirit of God (Eph. 5:20). It is an acknowledgment that all comes from God, and that he is doing good toward his own (2 Chron. 7:3; Pss. 106:1; 107:1). Thanksgiving looks for the goodness of God in all circumstances and all people (Col. 3:17; 1 Thess. 1:2; 2 Thess. 1:3). The continual giving of thanks reveals a heart and mind saturated with Christ.

Personal Implications

Take time to reflect on the implications of Ephesians 5:15–6:9 for your own life today. Consider what you have learned that might lead you to praise God, repent of sin, and trust in his gracious promises. Make notes below on the personal implications for your walk with the Lord of the (1) *Gospel Glimpses*, (2) *Whole-Bible Connections*, (3) *Theological Soundings*, and (4) this passage as a whole.

1. Gospel Glimpses

2. Whole-Bible Connections

3. Theological Soundings

4. Ephesians 5:15–6:9

As You Finish This Unit . . .

Take a moment now to ask for the Lord's blessing and help as you continue in this study of Ephesians. And take a moment also to look back through this unit of study, to reflect on some key things that the Lord may be teaching you—and perhaps to highlight and underline these things to review again in the future.

Definition

[1] **History of Salvation** – God's unified plan for all of history, to accomplish the salvation of his people. He accomplished this salvation plan in the work of Jesus Christ on earth by his life, crucifixion, burial, and resurrection (Eph. 1:10–12). The consummation of God's plan will take place when Jesus Christ comes again to establish the "new heavens and a new earth in which righteousness dwells" (2 Pet. 3:13).

Week 12: Standing Firm in the Real War

Ephesians 6:10–24

▲

In the final section of his letter to the Ephesians (6:10–24), Paul concludes with traditional personal greetings and with exhortations related to the letter carrier, Tychicus (vv. 21–22). He includes well-wishes of peace, love, faith, and grace, themes repeated throughout the letter (compare vv. 23–24 with 1:2; 2:7, 14; 3:21; 5:2; 6:16). Relative to the church as both a cosmic and an earthly entity, Paul closes the letter's instructions by expanding his understanding of the invisible challenge believers encounter in this world (1:21–22; 3:10; 4:9, 27; 5:16; 6:11–12, 16). Here Paul gives the largest explicit description of spiritual warfare within his writings.

The Big Picture

In 6:10–20, the believer's standing with the armor of God serves as a means of completing the church's gospel mission in the world. Paul revisits previously discussed ideas, including truth (4:21, 25), righteousness (4:24), the gospel of peace (2:14, 17; 4:3), faith (3:12, 17), salvation (2:5, 8), the working of the Spirit through the word (3:5), prayer (1:15–21; 3:14–21), and the mystery of the gospel (1:9; 3:3–4, 6, 9; 5:32). The apostle draws much of the imagery from Old Testament ideas—and from the armor of a Roman soldier—to speak of the believer's resources in Christ.

▶ Reflection and Discussion

Read through Ephesians 6:10–24, the passage for this week's study. Then review the following questions, taking notes on the final section of the letter to the Ephesians. (For further background, see the *ESV Study Bible*, pages 2273–2274; available online at esv.org.)

1. Cosmic Enemies That Require God's Armor (Eph. 6:10–13)

Paul urges the Ephesians to "be strong in the Lord and in the strength of his might" (6:10). Why does the nature of this war demand that we use the Lord's strength? How does the Devil fight (vv. 11–12)?

"Flesh and blood" is a figurative way of talking about *people*. If people are not the enemy, yet conflicts and the rejection of the gospel take place between people, how does one explain the nature of this struggle? What do the different types of powers of evil imply about the sort of warfare the church faces (6:12)?

Based on what Paul has said about activities "in the heavenly places" earlier in the epistle (1:3, 20; 2:6; 3:10), what sort of wrestling must believers do in the unseen realms (6:12)? How does wrestling with immaterial beings explain other conflict-related issues in Ephesians, such as ethnic rivalry (2:14), church disunity (4:3), mistreatment leading to anger (4:26, 31), and submission to authority (5:21)?

What does Paul mean by "the evil day"? How does one "stand firm" in the "whole armor" in that day?

way - truth - life

2. Soldier Imagery of God's Armor (6:14–17)

Paul list seven pieces of armor, including many that have Old Testament images in their background: belt (Isa. 11:5), breastplate (Isa. 59:17), feet related to the good news (Isa. 52:7), and garments of salvation (Isa. 61:10). How does the Old Testament background clarify the meaning of the "whole armor of God"?

belt - truth

It is possible to over-read Paul's imagery and think that the breastplate of righteousness protects one's heart or that the gospel of peace is necessary for walking because it deals with feet. This reading misunderstands the pieces of armor, missing the point Paul is making about behavior flowing from the power of Christ. How should you understand the role that the "belt of truth" plays in standing against the schemes of the Devil?

91

What activity of the believer is related to the "readiness given by the gospel of peace"? How does this activity operate in the believer's wrestling against evil forces?

How does the believer's faith counter the attacks of the Evil One? What habits related to the Word of God prepare the believer for wrestling against evil?

How do Paul's earlier discussions of the believer's salvation (Eph. 1:3–14; 2:4–10) inform one's understanding of the role of the "helmet of salvation" in fighting expressions of evil in the earthly realm?

3. Gospel Ministry in God's Armor (Eph. 6:18–20)

Looking to the previous working of the Spirit in Ephesians (5:18; 6:17), how does one pray "in the Spirit"? What might lead Paul to require "praying at all times" in order for the believer to stand?

Paul repeats "all" four times in 6:18 in instructing the believer on warfare prayer. What does each "all" say about the priority that prayer should have in the life of the believer? How does the call to "keep alert with all perseverance" give a greater understanding of the war strategy of the Devil?

How can a believer be faithful to pray for "all the saints"?

What does Paul face in this war that would make prayer necessary for him to declare the gospel "boldly" (6:19, 20)? How does this prayer request help the believer understand the danger of prayerlessness in the lives of individual believers and local churches?

Read through the following three sections on *Gospel Glimpses*, *Whole-Bible Connections*, and *Theological Soundings*. Then take time to consider the *Personal Implications* these sections may have for you.

Gospel Glimpses

THE LORD AS WARRIOR. The frail and finite nature of human existence ("flesh and blood"; Eph. 6:12) puts all people, including believers, at a severe disadvantage to spiritual rulers and powers who are not limited by bodily weaknesses or by the physical consequences of sin. The believer's hope of success in this war rests in Christ, who has provided the armor of God. By going to the cross and descending to the lower regions (4:8–10), Christ defeated the invisible powers who sought absolute rule over the domain of the earth (Col. 1:13). The believer finds salvation's victory—both present (Eph. 6:13) and final (Rom. 8:38–39)—in Christ our conqueror and in his finished work alone.

OUR LOVE FOR CHRIST. "Grace be with all who love our Lord Jesus Christ with love incorruptible" (Eph. 6:24). When God overcomes a sinner's heart by the power of the Spirit, Christ provides the believer a new heart that can respond to God in obedience. Love is vital to understanding the new relationship between God and the believer. It is "in love" that God has acted through Christ on behalf of the believer (2:4; 3:19). As Christ draws our affections into alignment with his will, we seek the good and glory of the God we love. Our love for him then flows into greater love for our fellow believers (1:15; 4:2, 15, 16; 5:2).

> ## Whole-Bible Connections

ANGELS AND DEMONS. The naturalistic worldview does not have room for personal, supernatural beings, despite the plethora of fictional literature and Hollywood productions portraying demonic characters in a battle for human souls. In contrast, the biblical worldview assumes the vibrant activity of both angels and demons. Angels are "ministers, who do his will" (Ps. 103:21). Demons, conversely, contribute to the opposition believers encounter in their life on earth. A day is coming when Christ will finally subjugate them (1 Cor. 15:24; 1 Pet. 3:22).

PRIORITY OF PRAYER. Many psalms portray the prayers of an individual sojourner or of an entire community seeking God (Pss. 40:1; 67:1; 123:1; 130:1), as do the books of history (2 Chron. 20:6–13; Nehemiah 9). Prayer was instrumental in the gospel's initial foray into the Roman Empire (Acts 1:14; 4:31; 6:4; 12:5; 13:3; 20:36). The invitation God offers the body of Christ to seek him in prayer is one of the amazing privileges of the believer. We can beseech the ruler of all things to act powerfully against invisible warring powers. Paul's examples, instructions, and requests relating to prayer reveal his belief in the believer's great need to prioritize this discipline.

> ## Theological Soundings

GOSPEL AMBASSADORS. "How are they to hear without someone preaching?" (Rom. 10:14). The church bears the task of proclaiming Christ to the world. The last command of Christ defines the goal of the church in the world (see Matt. 28:19–20; Luke 24:27–28; John 20:21; Acts 1:8). A fitting image of the believer's ministry of proclamation is that of ambassador. The believer acts as a representative of his homeland under the authority of his king. In heralding Christ, believers have the high honor of offering Christ as he invades history to win people to his kingdom.

ENCOURAGEMENT. Disappointments experienced during the daily conflict a believer faces in the world can lead to discouragement. But people whose hearts have been overcome by Christ's love have the ability to encourage one another with hope (1 Thess. 4:18; 5:11, 14). Encouraging words and deeds seek the benefit of the entire church (Col. 4:8). Encouragement is the fruit of having a trustworthy God who is a faithful refuge throughout all our trials (Heb. 6:18).

Personal Implications

Take time to reflect on the implications of Ephesians 6:10–24 for your own life today. Consider what you have learned that might lead you to praise God, repent of sin, and trust in his gracious promises. Make notes below on the personal implications for your walk with the Lord of the (1) *Gospel Glimpses*, (2) *Whole-Bible Connections*, (3) *Theological Soundings*, and (4) this passage as a whole.

1. Gospel Glimpses

2. Whole-Bible Connections

3. Theological Soundings

4. Ephesians 6:10–24

> ## As You Finish Studying Ephesians . . .

We rejoice with you as you finish studying the book of Ephesians! May this study become part of your Christian walk of faith, day-by-day and week-by-week throughout all your life. Now we would greatly encourage you to study the Word of God on a week-by-week basis. To continue your study of the Bible, we would encourage you to consider other books in the *Knowing the Bible* series, and to visit www.knowingthebibleseries.org.

Lastly, take a moment to look back through this study. Review the notes that you have written, and the things that you have highlighted or underlined. Reflect again on the key themes that the Lord has been teaching you about himself and about his Word. May these things become a treasure for you throughout your life—this we pray in the name of the Father, and the Son, and the Holy Spirit. Amen.

- The flesh Rom 7   what are you
- The word   doing today?
- The Enemy   How can I join
                   you?

3 battlegrounds - intertwine to
work against us.

I choose to believe _____